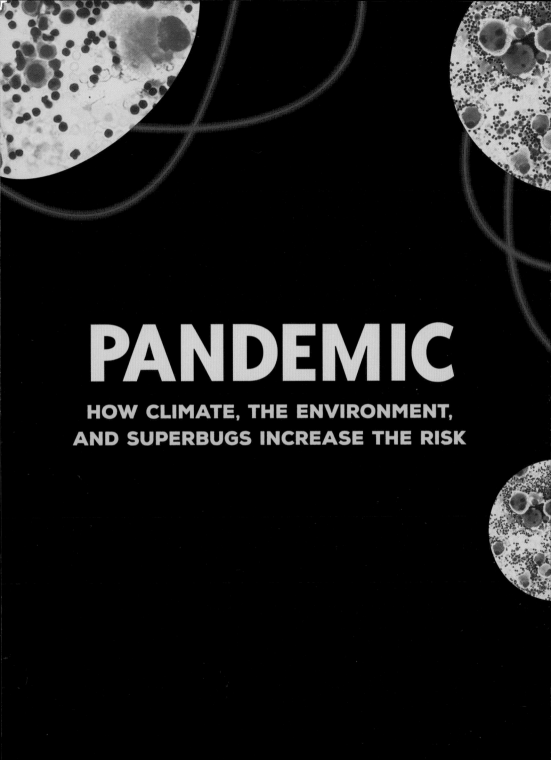

PANDEMIC

HOW CLIMATE, THE ENVIRONMENT, AND SUPERBUGS INCREASE THE RISK

PAND

EMIC

HOW CLIMATE, THE ENVIRONMENT, AND SUPERBUGS INCREASE THE RISK

CONNIE GOLDSMITH

TWENTY-FIRST CENTURY BOOKS / MINNEAPOLIS

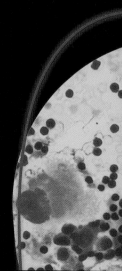

Twenty-First Century Books
A division of Lerner Publishing Group, Inc.
241 First Avenue North
Minneapolis, MN 55401 USA

For reading levels and more information, look up this title at www.lernerbooks.com.

Main body text set in Adobe Garamond Pro 11/15.
Typeface provided by Adobe Systems.

Library of Congress Cataloging-in-Publication Data

Names: Goldsmith, Connie, 1945– author.
Title: Pandemic : how climate, the environment, and superbugs increase the risk / by
    Connie Goldsmith.
Description: Minneapolis, MN : Twenty-First Century Books, a division of Lerner
    Publishing Group, Inc., [2018] | Audience: Ages 13–18. | Audience: Grades 9 to 12. |
    Includes bibliographical references and index.
Identifiers: LCCN 2017043693 (print) | LCCN 2017046752 (ebook) |
    ISBN 9781541524767 (eb pdf) | ISBN 9781512452150 (lb : alk. paper)
Subjects: LCSH: Epidemics—Juvenile literature. | Communicable diseases—Climatic
    factors—Juvenile literature. | Nature—Effect of human beings on—Juvenile
    literature.
Classification: LCC RA653.5 (ebook) | LCC RA653.5 .G65 2018 (print) | DDC
    614.4—dc23

LC record available at https://lccn.loc.gov/2017043693

Manufactured in the United States of America
1-42909-26514-1/8/2018

CONTENTS

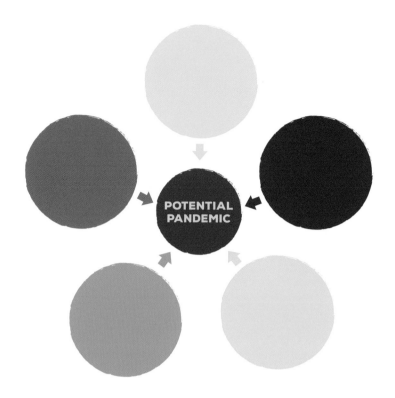

CHAPTER 1
BUGS IN THE NEWS

Over the last decades there have been about thirty newly emerging diseases that had the potential to be pandemics. It's not a matter of if there will be a global pandemic, it's just a matter of when and which virus and how bad.

—*Dr. Larry Brilliant, epidemiologist, 2017*

What do you think are the most dangerous animals in the world? Great white sharks? Poisonous snakes? People? Not even close. Believe it or not, mosquitoes are the most dangerous animals in the world. They are directly responsible for an estimated 725,000 human deaths each year. That is far more than the total number of deaths each year caused by people, snakes, sharks, and many other animals and insects combined.

A recent blood meal is visible in this mosquito's transparent gut. As it feeds, the mosquito can spread the malaria parasite and the viruses that cause Zika, dengue, and chikungunya.

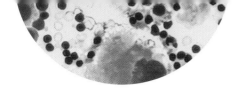

Why are mosquitoes so deadly? These flying disease factories carry more than a dozen lethal viruses and the malaria parasite. And these diseases are among the most dangerous in the world.

Pandemics (disease outbreaks that affect many people in many parts of the world) can bring the human race to its knees. History is filled with stories of such devastation. For example, in the fourteenth century, the Black Death wiped out at least 17 percent of the world's population. In modern times, epidemics (diseases that affect a large number of people in several places) have begun invading news reports around the globe.

In 1999 West Nile virus, spread by mosquitoes, reached the United States, and it has since spread to nearly every state. In 2003 severe acute respiratory syndrome (SARS) infected thousands of people and killed hundreds around the world. More recently, the Ebola and Zika viruses have spread death and tragedy on both sides of the Atlantic Ocean. Foodborne illnesses sicken an estimated forty-eight million Americans each year, killing thousands. And each year, like clockwork, one or more new strains of the flu begin to make the rounds.

No More Epidemics is an international campaign dedicated to preparing the world for epidemics and pandemics. Based on the world's population and infection rates of past pandemics, experts affiliated with the campaign predict that the world's next pandemic could kill between 180 and 360 million people during its first year alone. In 2017 many disease experts predicted that a pandemic is likely to occur within the next two or three decades. Some say it could be as soon as ten to fifteen years.

Several of the bacteria and viruses that have made headlines in the twenty-first century could cause the planet's next pandemic. New diseases are becoming more common, and old ones are reappearing more often. And the spread of all of these diseases has to do with human activity.

KNOW YOUR 'DEMICS

Epidemiologists—scientists who study diseases—rate the severity of a particular disease occurring at a given time in one of four ways:

- *Outbreaks* strike a limited number of people in a limited area and last a short time. Monkeypox, a distant relative of smallpox, appeared for the first time in the United States in 2003. During the two-month outbreak, more than seventy people in six midwestern states developed monkeypox.
- *Endemics* are diseases that are always present in a region. For example, malaria is endemic in several countries in Africa, such as Democratic Republic of the Congo, Nigeria, and Uganda.
- *Epidemics* hit a large number of people in several areas at the same time. In 2014–2015, scientists classified Ebola as an epidemic because it infected large numbers of people in three countries in West Africa.
- *Pandemics* affect many people in many parts of the world at the same time. For example, the Spanish flu of 1918–1919, which sickened millions of people around the world, was a true pandemic.

A BRIEF HISTORY OF PANDEMICS

Pandemics are not new. Ancient written records show that pandemics have occurred over many centuries. Historians believe that smallpox and bubonic plague likely triggered the earliest-recorded pandemics. Smallpox alone has caused an estimated one billion deaths since it first appeared around 10,000 BCE, although most cases occurred many centuries before medical science could positively identify it. Pandemics have changed the course of history, especially the three major historical pandemics: the Black Death, Spanish influenza, and human immunodeficiency virus (HIV), which causes acquired immunodeficiency syndrome (AIDS).

In the middle of the fourteenth century, the world population was about 450 million people. The bubonic plague, sometimes called the Black Death, killed between 17 and 44 percent of the world

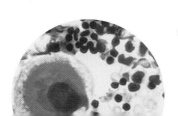

The National Institute of Allergy and Infectious Disease (NIAID) produced this digitally colored electron microscope image of *Yersinia pestis* (*Y. pestis*). The yellow *Y. pestis* bacteria are on parts of the digestive system of a flea (*in purple*).

population. In just four years—from 1347 to 1351—plague wiped out between one-third and one-half of all Europeans. *Yersinia pestis* (*Y. pestis*) is the bacteria responsible for plague. The bacteria live in fleas, which live on rats and other rodents. Italian traders returning from Asia brought the disease back with them, carried by flea-infected rats on their ships. Once a ship docked, the rats could move off the ship and enter the port. From there the rats, carrying the plague-infected fleas, spread into the city or town. The fleas infected local rats that lived close to people. The infected fleas moved between rats and people, easily infecting both.

Plague can infect the lungs, the blood, or, most commonly, the lymph nodes. A key part of the body's immune system, these small glands are scattered throughout the body to filter out bacteria.

WHAT'S IN A NAME?

Throughout history, scientists have come up with a way to classify and name every living thing using a system that is consistent within the scientific community around the world. Eight categories organize every plant, animal, and microorganism. These categories are domain, kingdom, phylum, class, order, family, genus, and species. Each category gets more and more specific. For example, all bacteria fall under the Bacteria domain, but a species name refers only to one kind of living thing. Latin-based terms name organisms within each of these categories.

In the eighteenth century, Swedish scientist Carolus Linnaeus created a scientific naming system called binomial nomenclature. Using the genus and species names for each organism, scientists can simply and clearly name every living thing. For example, the bacterium *Yersinia pestis* belongs to the genus *Yersinia* and the species *Yersinia pestis*. In scientific writing, the genus name is capitalized and can be abbreviated to use only the first letter, as in *Y. pestis*.

BACTERIA
(Domain)

EUBACTERIA
(Kingdom)

PROTEOBACTERIA
(Phylum)

GAMMAPROTEOBACTERIA
(Class)

ENTEROBACTERIALES
(Order)

YERSINIACEAE
(Family)

YERSINIA
(Genus)

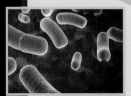

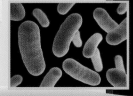

Black Death
(*Yersinia pestis*)

(Species)

Enterocolitis
(*Yersinia enterocolitica*)

When *Y. pestis* infects the lymph nodes, they swell into visible black lumps called buboes. These black buboes gave bubonic plague its name.

In the twenty-first century, plague still passes from fleas to rodents to people. Typically, fewer than ten Americans develop plague each year. Most are in New Mexico, Arizona, Colorado, and California, where wild rodents may carry plague-infected fleas. Nearly all infected people recover from the plague with antibiotic treatment.

In the twentieth century, another pandemic called Spanish flu ravaged Europe. This flu pandemic of 1918–1919 sickened up to one-third of the world's population and killed between fifty and one hundred million people. World War I (1914–1918) was nearly over, and many troops had been moving around the globe in crowded trains and ships. The flu—easily transmitted through droplets in the air when people sneeze, cough, or talk—traveled with them. This flu may have been the single worst pandemic of all time.

During the war, the governments of France, Britain, and the United States censored newspaper reports about sick troops. They feared that such reports would alert the enemy to a weakened army and lead to military disaster. When the flu reached Spain, a neutral country during this conflict, newspapers reported widely on the disease, especially when Spain's King Alfonso XIII fell seriously ill with the flu. For the first time, the rest of the world heard about the pandemic, incorrectly known from then on as the Spanish flu.

Scientists searched for the source of this pandemic for nearly a century. According to a 2014 *National Geographic* article, archival British and Canadian medical records suggest the Spanish flu originated in China. In 1918 Britain formed the Chinese Labour Corps to bring in workers from China and free up British soldiers for combat. The corps shipped ninety-four thousand Chinese workers to Europe, and historians believe the workers likely carried the flu there. Three thousand of the Chinese workers traveling across Canada to Europe became ill. Doctors, who held racist beliefs about

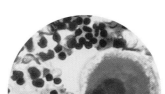

Influenza patients are treated in an army ward in Kansas in 1918. More than 600,000 Americans died from the Spanish flu pandemic.

the Chinese, said they were lazy, gave them castor oil for their sore throats, and sent them on their way. The Chinese workers arrived in England in January 1918 and were sent to France, where hundreds died of respiratory illness in a hospital.

The pandemic ended in 1919 as those who were infected either died or developed immunity to the virus. Since then several other flu pandemics and epidemics have occurred, though none have been as deadly as the Spanish flu. Each year flu viruses mutate into new strains that infect people. Some strains are deadlier than others. Through disease tracking, education, and vaccination, scientists and doctors hope to continue to control and respond to influenza so it does not cause another deadly pandemic.

The virus that causes AIDS was first identified in the early 1980s. Since then HIV has infected an estimated 70 million people around

A NIAID electron microscope image shows a red-colored cell that has been infected by HIV (*in yellow*). HIV attacks cells in the immune system so that the body can no longer fight off infection.

the world and killed about 35 million. The World Health Organization (WHO) is charged with monitoring and protecting the world's health. According to the organization, which is part of the United Nations (UN), 36.7 million people worldwide had HIV/AIDS by the end of 2015 and 1.1 million died of AIDS-related illnesses (such as infections and cancers) that year. The Centers for Disease Control and Prevention (CDC) reports that 1.1 million Americans are living with HIV, and one out of seven people with HIV don't know they have it. Even with improved treatments, this pandemic is still a serious global threat.

Researchers know that HIV began long before the 1980s. As scientists began tracking HIV's origins, evidence mounted that the deadly virus had circulated in sub-Saharan Africa for decades. Scientists believe the virus jumped from chimpanzees to humans in the early twentieth century, possibly in Cameroon. A disease that moves from animals to people is known as a zoonotic disease. In this case, the virus may have infected a human hunter when he killed a chimpanzee infected with simian immunodeficiency virus. The chimpanzee's blood likely splashed into an open wound on the hunter's body. Human and ape physiology (the processes and functions of the body) is similar enough that this virus could transfer to the hunter's body and adapt to become HIV. This man was HIV's index patient, the first person in the world known or believed to have contracted the disease. Scientists call him the cut hunter.

It can take years for symptoms of HIV infection to develop. Prize-winning science writer David Quammen traced the genetic origins of HIV by studying scientific literature and talking with researchers. Based on his findings, Quammen speculates on the spread of HIV from the index patient. The cut hunter, unknowingly infected with HIV, returned to his village in Cameroon and married. Perhaps an elephant or lion killed the cut hunter while the man was still young and seemingly healthy. His wife, infected with HIV through sexual relations with her husband, remarried. Through intercourse with her new husband, she passed HIV to him. After her death, perhaps in childbirth, her husband took a new wife, eventually infecting her as well. Children born of HIV-positive mothers may have the disease too.

Over time, the disease would have spread to more villagers. As they traveled to trade at other villages, some would have passed HIV along to more and more people through sexual encounters. Some modern researchers believe that well-intentioned medical care contributed to the spread of HIV/AIDS. European countries colonized parts of Africa in the early twentieth century and began health campaigns to treat diseases found in the colonies in the 1920s. At that time, all syringes were made of glass. They were expensive, scarce, and difficult to sterilize. Medical staff used the same syringes and needles repeatedly. One doctor injected more than five thousand people in two years using only six syringes without sterilizing them.

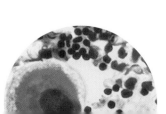

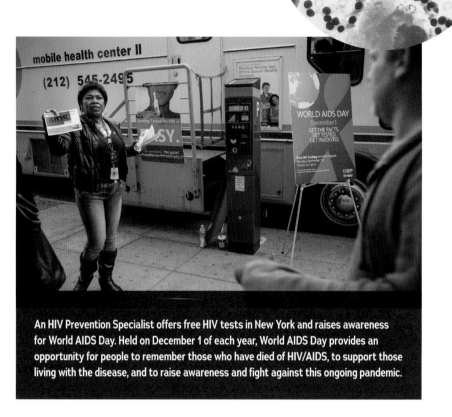

An HIV Prevention Specialist offers free HIV tests in New York and raises awareness for World AIDS Day. Held on December 1 of each year, World AIDS Day provides an opportunity for people to remember those who have died of HIV/AIDS, to support those living with the disease, and to raise awareness and fight against this ongoing pandemic.

In the 1960s, HIV/AIDS spread to Haiti. Belgium ruled the Democratic Republic of the Congo as its colony until 1960. Under Belgium, many in the Congo did not receive an education, so when the Congo gained independence, there was a shortage of doctors and teachers. The UN hired people from abroad to fill these positions. Many teachers came from Haiti. Likely one of these teachers brought HIV/AIDS back with them when they returned to Haiti. Within ten years, the disease spread to the United States. HIV/AIDS continued to spread to every region of the world. Yet two-thirds of new cases of HIV infection in the twenty-first century occur in sub-Saharan Africa. Experts believe that multiple factors—such as poverty, warfare, inadequate medical care, mobile workforces, polygyny (men having more than one wife), and genetics—can come together and make it difficult to control the spread of the disease.

GETTING TO KNOW BACTERIA

Bacteria (one-celled organisms) and viruses (tiny infectious agents that take over host cells) cause a wide variety of diseases. For example, bacteria cause cholera, Lyme disease, tetanus, and sexually transmitted diseases such as gonorrhea and syphilis. Viruses cause AIDS, Ebola, influenza, SARS, and Zika. No one knows if a bacteria or virus will trigger the next pandemic.

Every single human being carries around 3 pounds (1.4 kg) of bacteria in and on their bodies. While some bacteria may make us very sick or even kill us, most bacteria help us. In fact, we need bacteria. A delicate balance of helpful and dangerous bacteria exists inside the human body. Having the right bacteria in the right places helps to keep us healthy. For example, *Streptococcus viridans* lives harmlessly in our noses and throats, crowding out its dangerous cousin, *S. pneumoniae*, which can cause pneumonia and meningitis. Bacteria inside our intestines help us digest food, and several kinds of bacteria live on our skin, where they feast on dead skin cells. The bacteria we live with stimulate our immune systems to grow stronger, giving us a better chance of resisting harmful bacteria when they show up.

Bacteria come in five shapes: coccus (round bacteria that cause strep throat), bacillus (rod-shaped organisms such as the one that causes anthrax), vibrio (comma-shaped bacteria that cause cholera), spirochetes (corkscrew-shaped bacteria that cause syphilis), and spirilla (spiral-shaped bacteria that cause *Campylobacter* infection, a common type of food poisoning).

Many bacteria move with the help of taillike structures called flagella that propel them through fluids such as blood or water. The flagella help bacteria to move toward nutrients and away from toxic substances. Many species of bacteria also have pili (plural of pilus), small hairlike structures that help the bacteria attach to other cells and to surfaces such as the inside of a human throat. Pili can transfer genetic information between bacteria through conjugation. This

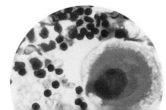

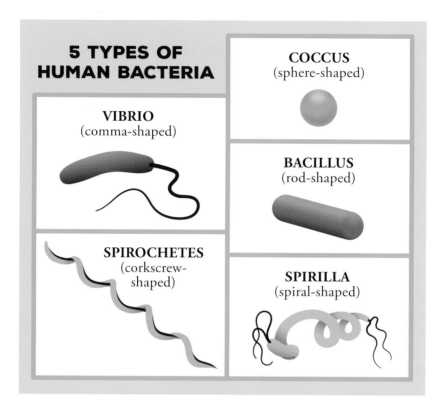

5 TYPES OF HUMAN BACTERIA

COCCUS
(sphere-shaped)

VIBRIO
(comma-shaped)

BACILLUS
(rod-shaped)

SPIROCHETES
(corkscrew-shaped)

SPIRILLA
(spiral-shaped)

process may provide the recipient bacteria with a genetic advantage to help it survive and thrive.

Some bacteria have a sticky outer layer called a capsule. Capsules keep these bacteria from drying out and dying. In healthy human immune systems, white blood cells attack and kill invading bacteria. But white blood cells can't destroy bacteria with capsules. Many bacteria that form capsules cause dangerous diseases.

Bacteria have cell walls that protect their internal structures. Inside the cell wall is a jellylike cytoplasm, which holds the following parts:

- *Ribosomes.* These food-making machines for bacteria take amino acids (organic compounds that combine to form proteins) from the cytoplasm and turn them into food using the bacterium's genetic instructions as a recipe.

- *Mitochondria*. They digest nutrients to provide cells with energy.
- *Chromosomes*. They hold the genetic information—the deoxyribonucleic acid (DNA) or ribonucleic acid (RNA)—that bacteria need to reproduce. The DNA and RNA are in a region of the cell called the nucleoid. DNA is a substance in cells that carries the genes that control all aspects of an organism's reproduction, appearance, and survival. For example, in humans, genes determine height, eye color, and many other physical traits. RNA's main role is to carry instructions from DNA to other

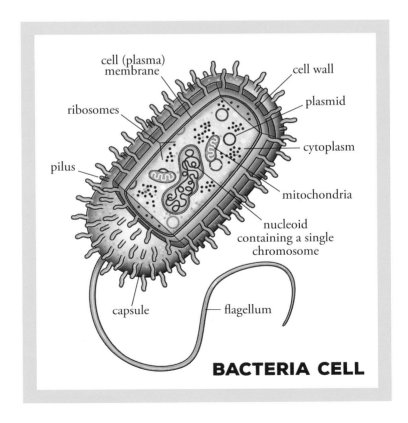

BACTERIA CELL

parts of the cell. Chemically, RNA is nearly identical to DNA, but it has only one strand of chemical base units, while DNA has two.

- *Plasmids*. Some bacteria carry these circular strands of DNA in their cytoplasm. Bacteria may transfer plasmids to one another through conjugation. The genetic information in plasmids may give a bacterium a genetic advantage such as helping it to become resistant to antibiotics.

A bacterium reproduces by dividing into two identical cells. Under the right conditions, some bacteria can divide every twenty to thirty minutes. In eight hours, a bacterium can produce 16,777,216 bacteria! Bacteria move. They reproduce. They require food to survive, and most require oxygen.

GETTING TO KNOW VIRUSES

Bacteria are living organisms. Viruses are something else. Not really alive yet not quite dead, viruses are the zombies of the microscopic world. Viruses can't carry out any of the activities that define life. They can't move or reproduce by themselves. Viruses don't need food or oxygen to live. What they need is a living host cell.

Viruses are much smaller and structurally much simpler than bacteria. While scientists can see bacteria under a simple, low-power microscope, they must have a high-powered electron microscope to see viruses. Viruses have a protective protein shell called a capsid that surrounds one or two strands of genetic material. Some viruses also have an outer envelope composed of lipids (compounds such as fat and oil that do not dissolve in water). That's all. No ribosomes. No nucleoid. No plasmids.

On its own, a virus is an inactive bundle of genes searching for a host cell. The sole mission of a virus is to get inside a cell and

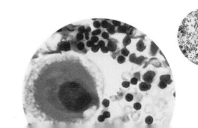

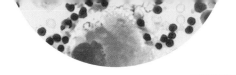

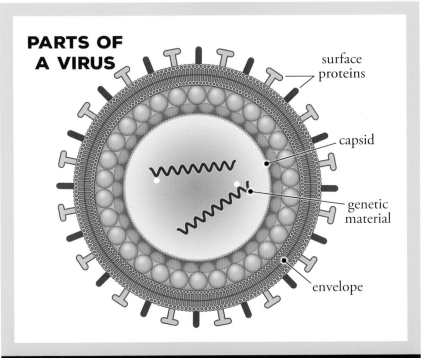

PARTS OF A VIRUS

surface proteins

capsid

genetic material

envelope

Virus envelopes include surface proteins that help the virus attach to a host cell. These proteins often look like a fringe of spikes or knobs around the virus.

turn it into a factory to produce new viruses. Viruses replicate at warp speed because they are so much simpler than bacteria. It takes only minutes to attack a living cell, gain control of its reproductive machinery, and churn out a new generation of viruses. Each daughter virus quickly moves on to infect other cells.

Such rapid replication means that viruses have a very high rate of mutation, a random and spontaneous change in an organism's genetic code. Viruses contain *either* RNA *or* DNA, unlike higher life-forms such as bacteria, which contain both. When a genetic mutation occurs in a DNA virus (or a bacterium), the cell usually repairs itself before it replicates, so that new cells don't carry the mutation. But RNA viruses such as those that cause HIV, Ebola, and influenza are too small to hold a cell repair program. So mutations that don't kill the RNA virus will be passed on to the next generation. RNA viruses are especially dangerous because of their constant and uncontrolled mutations. Some genetic mutations help viruses better adapt to their environment or make them more dangerous to people.

LOOKING AHEAD

Whether bacteria or virus, most infectious diseases are zoonotic, jumping from animals to people. According to Dr. Ali S. Khan, dean of the College of Public Health at the University of Nebraska Medical Center, 70 to 80 percent of emerging infectious diseases come to us from animals. Nearly half of them are viral diseases. Other infectious diseases, such as foodborne illnesses, sicken us from bacteria we introduce through careless human behavior. For example, unsanitary handling of raw meat and vegetables can contaminate food products. Khan says, "We humans act like we own the planet, when really it's the microbes [bacteria, viruses, and parasites] and the insects that run

EMERGING AND REEMERGING DISEASES

Scientists use the terms *emerging* and *reemerging* to help describe diseases. Emerging diseases are generally those to which humans have not previously been exposed. These include SARS and some strains of the flu. Other emerging diseases may have occurred for years but were unrecognized or unnamed. Ebola and Lyme disease are also examples of emerging diseases.

A reemerging disease is one that once was under control but has become more widespread or resistant to treatment. Examples of reemerging diseases include cholera and dengue, which are spreading, and malaria and tuberculosis, which are increasingly difficult to treat.

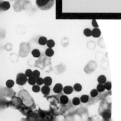

things. One way they remind us who's in charge is by transmitting disease, often with the help of small animals, including rodents or bats."

Scientists do not yet know what will cause the next pandemic. It could be a new bacterium that resists all available medications. Or it could be a mutated virus to which people have no immunity. What scientists and epidemiologists do know is that human activity is largely responsible for the spread of disease. Air travel, climate change, disruption of animal habitats, human crowding, and overuse of antibiotics have all contributed to the increase of zoonotic diseases in recent years.

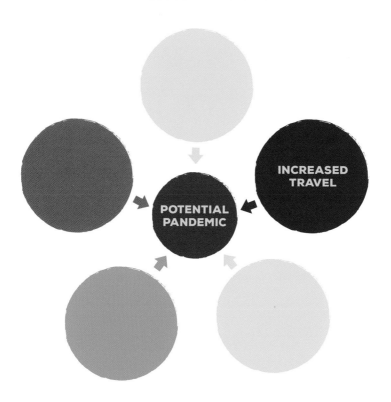

CHAPTER 2

Bugs on a Plane

Within twenty-four hours, the SARS virus . . . had spread to five
countries; ultimately, SARS appeared in thirty-two countries.
Thanks to the miracle of air travel, one infected man seeded a
global outbreak.

—Sonia Shah, science journalist and author, 2016

On an average day, more than eight million people fly on
commercial planes. Experts predict the number of people
traveling by air will double over the next twenty years. And these
millions of people take more than their suitcases, swimsuits, and

The Beijing Capital International Airport is the world's second-busiest airport, handling more than 94 million passengers in 2016. With millions of people traveling through airports each day, bacteria and viruses can spread easily and quickly around the world.

snowboards along when they travel. They also take bacteria and viruses with them. Pathogens—disease-causing microbes—don't have wings or legs, so they can't travel on their own. Instead, they hitch a ride to their final destination. Often that ride is with a passenger who is sitting for hours inside a crowded plane with poor air circulation.

Prolonged close contact during air travel greatly increases the risk of one person passing a microbe to others. Air travel also often includes stops and layovers along the way, and each of those layovers and flight changes increases the time that a person can pick up—and spread—an infection. It also increases the number of people to whom a traveler is exposed and to whom that traveler can spread the infection.

Imagine you're sitting in the middle row on a six-hour flight from San Francisco to New York. The person seated to your right seems to have a cold and coughs all the way, exposing you to that illness. But what's really scary is the possibility that the person to your left is carrying a dangerous microbe without even knowing it. The time between when a person becomes infected with a microbe and when symptoms begin is the incubation period of that microbe. Dr. Mary E. Wilson is a professor of epidemiology and biostatistics and a medical editor for *Health Information for International Travel*, a CDC publication. She says, "The elimination of . . . barriers, especially by long-distance air transport, means that humans can reach almost any part of the Earth today within the incubation period for most microbes that cause disease in humans." So people can unknowingly spread dangerous infections during the incubation period.

In 2009 air travel contributed to the spread of a new strain of flu known as H1N1, or swine flu. H1N1 started in Mexico in March 2009 after the flu season there would normally have been over. Flu is typically most dangerous for the elderly, but H1N1 hit children and young people harder. One month later, H1N1 reached the United States, then Canada, and it soon spread to seventy-four countries. On June 11, 2009, Dr. Margaret Chan, then director-general of WHO, said, "The world is now at the start of the 2009 influenza pandemic. . . . No previous pandemic has been detected so early or watched so closely, in real-time, right at the very beginning."

Former president Barack Obama declared H1N1 a national emergency in the United States on October 24, 2009. A laboratory-related delay slowed the release of the newly developed H1N1 vaccine, leaving millions of Americans without protection. Between April 2009 and April 2010, nearly 61 million people around the world developed the H1N1 flu. Experts estimated the global death toll of H1N1 to be 284,000 people, about fifteen times more than the number of actual laboratory-confirmed deaths.

CASE STUDY: SARS

Kwan Sui-chu, a seventy-eight-year-old Canadian grandmother, didn't know that she was carrying the first new disease of the twenty-first century when she flew from Hong Kong back home to Toronto, Ontario, in February 2003. Although she felt well, a dangerous virus lurked deep within her lungs. Kwan and her husband had spent two weeks visiting their sons in Hong Kong. They had checked into the Metropole Hotel for one night on February 21 before their flight home. The reasonably priced hotel drew many international tourists.

Back in Toronto, Kwan returned to the apartment she shared with family members. Two days later, she developed a high fever, muscle aches, and a cough. Kwan's doctor prescribed rest and antibiotics, but that didn't help. Kwan died at home a few days later of what her doctor said was a heart attack. But Kwan died of severe acute respiratory syndrome, a disease spread by coughing, sneezing, and touching contaminated surfaces. Kwan infected five other family members before the new disease even had a name.

However, SARS didn't start with Kwan. The first cases of the mysterious new illness broke out among people who had purchased wildlife from a wet market in Guangzhou, a city of more than thirteen million people in China's Guangdong Province. Vendors at these markets sold a huge variety of live wildlife for food and butchered it for customers on the spot (thus the name *wet market*). Cages crammed with bats, snakes, foxes, rats, raccoon dogs, ferret badgers, and civets were stacked on top of one another. The animals at the market were unlikely to be near one another in the wild. But in the wet market they were. This allowed pathogens such as the SARS virus to pass from animal to animal and from them to people.

Dozens of cases of the disease broke out in Guangzhou during November and December 2002 and into January 2003. The still-unnamed disease caused headaches, high fever, severe coughing, and bloody sputum from the lungs. At its worst, the disease damaged the

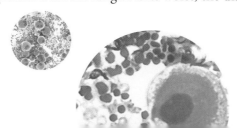

lungs so they couldn't provide enough oxygen to the body. At first, Chinese authorities didn't acknowledge the new disease. Instead, the Guangzhou media advised people to spray vinegar into the air and onto surfaces in their homes to kill the virus. Citizens rushed to buy vinegar, flu medication, and antibiotics. None of these precautions helped.

By early February, SARS had sickened more than three hundred people and killed five in Guangzhou. So on February 10, 2003, China finally reported the new disease to WHO. Later that month, Dr. Liu Jianlun, who had treated SARS patients in Guangzhou, went to Hong Kong for a family wedding. He checked into Hong Kong's Metropole Hotel on the same day and on the same floor as the Kwans. Liu became very ill and went to a Hong Kong hospital the next day. Liu probably infected Kwan and dozens of other people at the hotel overnight by coughing and sneezing in hotel hallways and elevators. Soon guests at the hotel became ill. Health-care workers at the local hospitals who cared for them became ill. Like Kwan, many infected people traveled from Hong Kong and gave SARS to people along the way and at their final destinations.

Scientists later determined that SARS started when horseshoe bats infected animals a few months or years before the disease broke out in Guangzhou. The bats carried evidence of a new type of coronavirus (a family of RNA viruses named for their crown-like shape). SARS is a distant relative of the coronavirus that causes about 15 percent of common colds in humans. The ferret badgers and civets in the Guangzhou market seemed to be especially vulnerable to the virus. As the virus spread among them, it likely mutated and became easily transmissible to humans.

In March 2003, Dr. Gro Harlem Brundtland, then director-general of WHO, said, "This syndrome, SARS, is now a worldwide health threat." Due to the volume of international air travel, cases soon spread to the United States, Vietnam, Taiwan, Singapore, and several countries in Europe, as well as to Canada and mainland China. By the

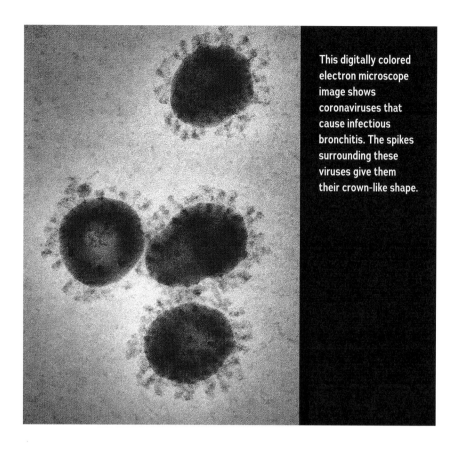

This digitally colored electron microscope image shows coronaviruses that cause infectious bronchitis. The spikes surrounding these viruses give them their crown-like shape.

end of 2003, SARS had sickened more than eight thousand people and killed about eight hundred.

SARS is highly contagious. During the 2003 epidemic, it killed nearly one out of every ten people it infected. Yet it didn't turn into a global pandemic. Why not? First, scientists identified the virus quickly once it became public. Well-equipped, well-staffed hospitals treated most of the patients. China closed schools and put thousands of people in quarantine (isolation from other people) to stop the spread of SARS. Experts quickly traced the contacts of each sick person to discover whom they might have infected and put those people in quarantine as well.

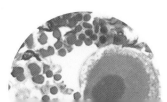

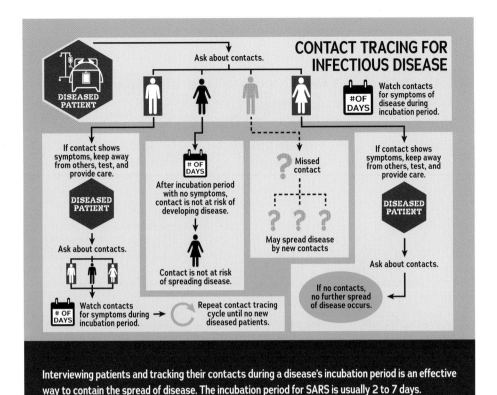

CONTACT TRACING FOR INFECTIOUS DISEASE

DISEASED PATIENT

Ask about contacts.

Watch contacts for symptoms of disease during incubation period.

#OF DAYS

If contact shows symptoms, keep away from others, test, and provide care.

DISEASED PATIENT

Ask about contacts.

OF DAYS Watch contacts for symptoms during incubation period.

Repeat contact tracing cycle until no new diseased patients.

OF DAYS After incubation period with no symptoms, contact is not at risk of developing disease.

Contact is not at risk of spreading disease.

? Missed contact

? ? ? May spread disease by new contacts

If contact shows symptoms, keep away from others, test, and provide care.

DISEASED PATIENT

Ask about contacts.

If no contacts, no further spread of disease occurs.

Interviewing patients and tracking their contacts during a disease's incubation period is an effective way to contain the spread of disease. The incubation period for SARS is usually 2 to 7 days.

Lastly, the symptoms of SARS seem to appear *before* the person is infectious. So SARS patients can be identified and isolated before they release the SARS virus into the air with every cough. This is different from many other diseases. For example, with the flu, people feel well but are infectious before symptoms appear. They spread the flu virus a full day or more before they realize they're sick.

CASE STUDY: MONKEYPOX

People are not the only passengers on commercial planes. Nearly one and a half billion live animals—including mammals, birds, fish, reptiles, amphibians, and insects—reached the United States from countries around the world between 2000 and 2006. And those are just the legal imports. The Wildlife Conservation Society estimates that illegal animal trade is a $6 billion global industry. They think that tens of thousands of other animals, including tigers, monkeys, and exotic food animals, were illegally smuggled into the United States in private planes and boats during that time.

Whether legal or illegal, any of those animals may carry a new disease or a disease never before seen in the United States. That happened when a shipment of African rodents, including large rodents known as Gambian rats, brought monkeypox to the United States in 2003. On Mother's Day of that year, Tammy Kautzer took her three-year-old daughter Schyan to a swap meet in Wausau, Wisconsin. A pet dealer there sold two young prairie dogs to Kautzer.

Two days later, Kautzer thought one of the prairie dogs seemed like it had a cold. Kautzer took the prairie dog to the vet. The vet diagnosed a swollen lymph node and prescribed antibiotics. The animal's viruses infected several people at the vet's office that day.

Left to right: Schyan, Steve, and Tammy Kautzer were quarantined at their home after contracting monkeypox. Tammy holds Chuckles, the prairie dog that survived the infection. The family decided to keep Chuckles as they believed they were immune from contracting monkeypox again.

The prairie dog died at the Kautzer home a few days later, but not before he'd bitten Schyan's finger. Schyan developed a fever of 103°F (39°C), and fluid-filled bumps appeared on her skin. Kautzer took her daughter to the doctor. Two days later, Schyan was admitted to the hospital. Doctors eventually diagnosed Schyan with monkeypox, a viral disease related to smallpox that had never been seen in the United States before it sent Schyan to the hospital. Schyan's parents—and Chuckles, the other prairie dog—both got mild cases of monkeypox as well. All recovered completely.

CDC disease detectives quickly traced the outbreak to a batch of several hundred infected rodents shipped from Ghana to a pet distributor in Texas. The distributor—who did not know the animals were sick—sent the rodents to Illinois. There, a pet dealer housed them with American prairie dogs, which are often sold as pets, like the ones the Kautzers bought. With no natural immunity to monkeypox, the prairie dogs quickly caught the disease from the African rodents and became ill. When people purchased the prairie dogs as pets, the animals and the people got sick too. By the end of the outbreak, seventy-one people in six midwestern states had developed monkeypox. All had contact with infected prairie dogs. Several were hospitalized.

Two strains of monkeypox circulate in remote areas of central and West Africa. The most dangerous strain kills up to 10 percent of those infected. The milder strain is the one that reached the United States. To prevent a widespread epidemic, US health officials quarantined people and animals that had been exposed to the monkeypox. They also gave the smallpox vaccination to vets, health-care workers, and others at high risk of infection.

If someone had released just one infected prairie dog into the wild, monkeypox could have spread to millions of American prairie dogs and other wildlife such as mice, squirrels, and porcupines. The disease could have decimated wildlife and spread to people. To prevent another

BUGS IN TIRES

In the world's global economy, manufactured goods are always on the move. They can be a source of dangerous infections too. Starting in the 1960s, millions of used tires made their way each year into the United States. Often the tires came from Japan, which for decades was the world's largest exporter of used tires. The tires arrived in giant containers on giant cargo ships. And inside tiny puddles of water in these used tires were millions of mosquitoes, their eggs, and their larvae. When workers unloaded the tires, they also unknowingly unloaded new mosquito species never before found in the United States.

The United States imports far fewer used tires than it once did. But the damage is done—the mosquitoes are here. *Aedes aegypti* and *Aedes albopictus* are two species that probably hitchhiked to the United States in tires. Epidemiologists aren't certain if these mosquitoes were carrying diseases when they arrived. But these two species of mosquitoes inhabit a wide area of the United States, and they transmit a variety of dangerous viruses. (Not every species of mosquito carries and spreads disease.) So if—or when—a virus normally transmitted by these two species reaches the United States, *Ae. aegypti* and *Ae. albopictus* are already on the ground and able to spread it.

outbreak, the CDC quickly banned the import of all African rodents. As Khan said, "In the age of air travel, a disease anywhere can very quickly become a disease everywhere."

COULD THIS BE THE NEXT PANDEMIC?

Could SARS cause the next pandemic? Possibly. If SARS moves to humans from bats or other animals, the disease could spread rapidly again. Several organizations are working on a vaccine to prevent SARS in case the virus returns. Such a vaccine could be tested for safety, but scientists can't know if a vaccine actually prevents SARS in people unless the virus returns.

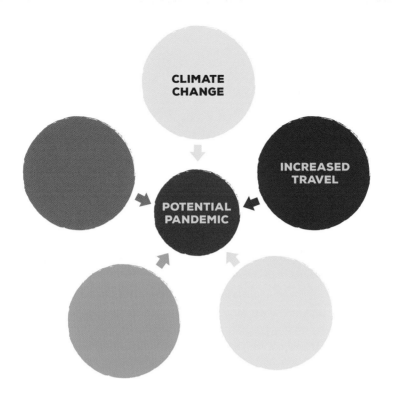

CHAPTER 3

Climate Change, Insects, and Animals

A longer warm-weather season and changing rainfall patterns are allowing the insects that can transmit disease to humans to thrive for longer periods each year—and to simultaneously move into broader areas.

—Kim Knowlton, senior scientist, National Resource Defense Council, 2015

Floodwaters surround office buildings in Houston, Texas, in 2017, following Hurricane Harvey. Climate change may cause more hurricanes and flooding, which may lead to increased mosquito populations.

The National Aeronautics and Space Administration (NASA) reported that 2016 was the hottest year since modern weather recordkeeping began in 1880. Gavin Schmidt, director of NASA's Goddard Institute for Space Studies, said that 2016 "is remarkably the third record year in a row. . . . We don't expect record years every year, but the ongoing long-term warming trend is clear." The trend continued in 2017. The first ten months of the year were the second hottest on record.

Earth's average temperature has risen about 2.0°F (1.1°C) since the late nineteenth century. That may not seem like a big increase, but small changes affect the world in big ways. Hot, dry weather can lead to prolonged droughts and food shortages. Temperature increases also cause the ice in the Arctic and Antarctic to melt more quickly.

CLIMATE CHANGE AND GLOBAL WARMING

While people sometimes use the terms *climate change* and *global warming* interchangeably, NASA says the two terms describe different phenomena. Climate change refers to ongoing changes in average temperature, humidity, and rainfall around the world. Global warming, on the other hand, is a part of climate change that refers to the trend of increasing temperature on Earth since the early twentieth century. Climate change and global warming are both caused mostly by burning fossil fuels, which adds heat-trapping gases to Earth's atmosphere.

For example, in July 2017, an iceberg nearly the size of Delaware broke away from the Antarctic ice shelf and drifted into the ocean. Sea levels of some American coasts have risen by 8 inches (20 cm) over the past fifty years.

A 2017 report by the Union of Concerned Scientists predicted that by 2035, about 170 American cities on the East and West Coasts as well as the Gulf Coast will experience chronic flooding leading to the loss of land and homes. Increased rainfall, which is associated with climate change, can cause devastating flooding such as the 50 inches (127 cm) that fell on Texas and Louisiana during Hurricane Harvey in 2017. All of these changes can cause infectious diseases to spread more rapidly and to sicken more people.

ZOMBIE MICROBES

Much of the Arctic region is particularly vulnerable to warming. As the ice that once reflected the sun's heat back into space melts, the land and ocean in the Arctic can absorb more of the sun's heat. "[The temperature] is rising about three times faster in the Arctic than in the

Reindeer are very important to the Nenets of Siberia. Nenets travel year-round along the migration routes of the reindeer and use reindeer for food, tents, clothing, and tools. Along with releasing deadly pathogens, climate change has led to changes in migration patterns, leaving less available food for the reindeer. As reindeer go hungry and die from disease, the Nenets face difficulties in preserving their lifestyle.

rest of the world," Dr. Birgitta Evengard of Sweden's Umea University said. "And that means the ice is melting, and the permafrost is thawing." Permafrost is a layer of soil and rock that normally remains permanently frozen. In some Arctic locations, the average winter temperature is –13°F (–25°C), and the permafrost is more than 1,000 feet (304 m) deep—about the height of New York City's Empire State Building.

High above the Arctic Circle, the nomadic Nenets live in a remote region of Siberia (a region of northern Russia) called the Yamal Peninsula. In a study published in 2011, scientists from the Russian Academy of Sciences predicted that thawing Arctic permafrost could release old and new zoonoses. The scientists' predictions came true in the summer of 2016 when temperatures on the peninsula soared to 95°F (35°C) for months at a time. Permafrost began melting in the extraordinarily hot weather, and long-dormant (inactive) pathogens began to emerge. Some scientists are calling these pathogens zombie microbes. They were once seemingly dead but are alive again.

For example, anthrax bacteria form hardy spores—tough protective shells that can survive for one hundred years or more. When temperatures heat up, the bacteria come out of dormancy and are infectious once again. During the 2016 summer in the Yamal Peninsula, anthrax spores emerged and spread, sickened nearly one hundred people, and killed a twelve-year-old boy as well as more than two thousand reindeer and several sled dogs. Russian scientists believe that thawing permafrost exposed a reindeer carcass that had died of anthrax seventy-five years before. Wind likely scattered the infectious spores across the tundra. Living reindeer in the area foraged for food, ate anthrax-contaminated plants, became infected, and died.

The local government acted quickly to control the anthrax outbreak and prevent additional loss of human and animal life. "People were evacuated, dogs put to sleep [and our tents] and sledges . . . were set on fire," Alexey Nenyanga, a Nenet reindeer herder, said. "Nothing was left. . . . In our world, if a herder is left without reindeer, he has nothing else." Because the Nenet way of life is tied directly to reindeer, the Russian government started a program to vaccinate reindeer against anthrax. By August 2017, seventy thousand reindeer in the Yamal Peninsula had been vaccinated.

But anthrax may not be the only infectious disease the thawing Arctic permafrost exposes. In 2012 the *New England Journal of Medicine* published an article describing DNA fragments from a previously unknown strain of smallpox. Scientists had found them in three-hundred-year-old human mummies frozen in Siberian permafrost.

Scientists have also found giant viruses in Siberian permafrost that are at least thirty thousand years old. Giant viruses are a class of complex viruses that are large enough to see under an ordinary microscope. Researchers reported in 2013 that they had revived the Siberian giant viruses in the lab and tested their impact on one-celled amoebas, and on animal cells and human cells. The viruses infected the amoebas, but not the animal or human cells. Even so, in 2015 researchers warned that the discovery of the new strain of smallpox and the giant viruses in permafrost are reasons to be concerned about climate change. Evengard said, "So we really don't know what's buried up there [in the Siberian permafrost]." Could thawing of the permafrost bring back smallpox? Anthrax? Could newly identified giant viruses bring unknown diseases to humankind? It seems possible.

MEET THE VECTORS

Vectors are the living organisms, typically biting and stinging insects, that carry disease-causing pathogens from one host to another. Ticks carry the bacteria that cause Lyme disease, and mosquitoes carry viruses that cause West Nile, Zika, dengue, and chikungunya. Mosquitoes also carry the parasites that cause malaria. Fleas carry plague bacteria. These insects spread disease when they bite people and animals. For example, female mosquitoes must bite people or animals to get protein from blood so their eggs can develop. Viruses and malaria parasites live in mosquito saliva. Mosquitoes inject their saliva when they bite. The saliva has an anesthetic effect so people don't feel the bite at first. The saliva is also a blood thinner so blood won't clot as the mosquito feeds. Mosquitoes bite four to five people with each blood meal, and they take three to four blood meals during their two-week life span. An infected mosquito could quickly infect a dozen or more people.

According to a 2016 report from the US Global Change Research Program, "Climate change is expected to alter the geographic and seasonal distributions of existing vectors and vector-borne diseases." Temperatures could climb by as much as 2°F to 3°F (1.1°C to 1.7°C) by 2050, according to the report. Rising temperatures contribute to the

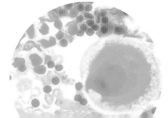

spread of many infectious diseases around the world. Dr. Ilissa Ocko, a climate scientist with the Environmental Defense Fund, said, "There are three ways . . . that warmer weather may be contributing to the . . . crisis: 1) Hotter temperatures make mosquitoes hungrier; 2) Warm air incubates the virus faster; and 3) Mosquito territory expands as the climate warms."

Rising temperatures allow mosquitoes and ticks to move into areas that have become warmer. Mosquitoes are cold-blooded and die or hibernate at temperatures less than 50°F (10°C). They prefer temperatures over 80°F (27°C) and can be active to about 104°F (40°C) degrees. A change of even a couple of degrees can affect their life span. The time between when the mosquito lays her eggs and when they hatch decreases as temperatures rise. Since 1980 the mosquito season, the time when mosquitoes hatch or come out of hibernation until temperatures cool and they die off or begin to hibernate again, has increased by five days in 125 American cities and by one month in 10 cities. So more mosquitoes that can make us sick are around for a longer time.

The report on climate change said that ticks likely would become active for longer periods and spread to more areas as temperatures rise. Ticks thrive in a humidity of 85 percent or more and temperatures above 45°F (7.2°C). So the tick life span will lengthen, which will lead to a longer breeding and egg-laying season. Then more ticks can bite and infect more people and animals.

LYME DISEASE AND TICK VECTORS

Usually doctors are the first to notice a new disease. But in 1975, two mothers called attention to bizarre symptoms in their children. It started when one mother in Lyme, Connecticut, took her children to several doctors, trying to find the cause for their painful swollen joints. One month later, another mother called the Connecticut Department of Public Health to report an outbreak of similar symptoms among children in her neighborhood. Joint problems often occur in older people with arthritis but are extremely rare in young children.

Soon doctors found what seemed to be severe arthritis in thirty-nine children and a dozen adults in the small town of Lyme. Some people recalled having a red circular rash before the joint pains began. Doctors knew that tick bites cause such rashes, often called a bull's-eye rash because of the shape and color. Doctors concluded that ticks in the region were carrying a disease that was new to the United States. They named it Lyme disease.

Lyme disease is the most common vector-borne illness in the United States. Doctors have reported it in nearly every state, according to the Lyme Disease Association. The CDC reported 36,429 confirmed and probable cases of Lyme disease in forty-seven states in 2016 (the last year for which complete numbers are available). Researchers estimate that up to 376,000 new cases occur annually. Two environmental drivers make Lyme disease one of the fastest-growing infectious diseases in the United

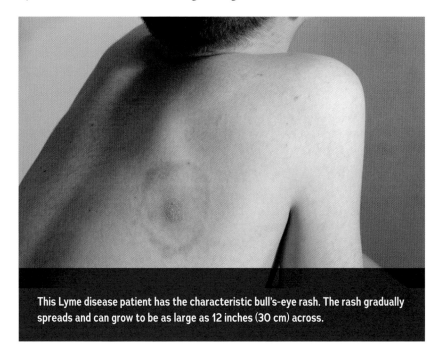

This Lyme disease patient has the characteristic bull's-eye rash. The rash gradually spreads and can grow to be as large as 12 inches (30 cm) across.

States. First, because of warmer temperatures, ticks have longer breeding seasons and are moving into areas that were previously too cold for them. Second, as the number of woodsy suburban housing developments around the country grows, families are exposed to more ticks.

The ticks that carry Lyme disease climb to the top of tall grasses often found near and in wooded areas or other places with thick vegetation. When a person brushes by, the tick climbs onto its new meal ticket. If not removed, the tick may feed on human blood for several days before dropping off. The longer the tick is attached, the greater the risk that it will transmit Lyme disease (and other diseases ticks carry) to that person.

About eight out of ten people with Lyme disease develop a rash that often—but not always—forms a bull's-eye pattern within a month. Flulike symptoms such as fever, chills, fatigue, and body aches occur. Later symptoms include joint pain, bone pain, and problems with the nervous system such as headaches, nerve pain, inflammation of the brain and spinal cord, and memory problems. Lyme disease can infect the heart, causing chest pain and fainting.

If doctors diagnose Lyme disease early enough, antibiotics can often cure it. Other people may have chronic Lyme disease, with symptoms that last for months or years, despite antibiotic treatment. Tens of thousands of people live with chronic pain and fatigue. Many of them believe that Lyme disease causes their symptoms. However, mainstream doctors and the CDC think these patients have a post-treatment syndrome or another disease entirely. Up to one-third of people infected with Lyme disease are ill for a long time. Experts disagree on how to diagnose it, how to define it, and for how long to treat it.

WEST NILE VIRUS

The United States has some of the best mosquito-control programs in the world. Many people take steps to avoid being bitten. They wear long-sleeved shirts and pants as well as mosquito repellent. However,

HOW TO REMOVE A TICK SAFELY

You can avoid ticks in areas with tall grasses and many trees, where they might live. Wear long-sleeved shirts, long pants rather than shorts, and shoes and socks instead of sandals. Wear a hat and use insect repellent on your skin and clothing. Examine your skin and clothing when you get home. Follow these steps if you find a tick on a person or pet:

- Don't touch the tick. Don't burn it with a match or cover it with Vaseline.
- Use fine-tipped tweezers to grasp the tick as close to the skin's surface as possible.
- Pull upward with steady, even pressure. Twisting or jerking the tweezers can cause the tick's mouthparts to break off and remain in the skin, which could cause an infection.
- Use an iodine scrub, alcohol, or soap and water to clean the bite area. Wash your hands well with soap and water after removing the tick.
- Save the tick in a plastic bag or small bottle in case your doctor wants to see it. If your doctor does not need to see the tick, douse it with alcohol and discard it inside a sealed plastic bag or flush it down the toilet.

cases of mosquito-borne infections such as West Nile virus, dengue, and chikungunya are likely to climb as warming temperatures increase the territorial range of the mosquitoes that carry those viruses. According to a 2015 forum on microbial threats sponsored by the Institute of Medicine (later called the National Academy of Medicine), "Global environmental change allowed the formerly range-restricted dengue, chikungunya, and West Nile viruses to reemerge among major populations worldwide."

The West Nile virus was first identified in Uganda in 1937. It reached the United States in 1999 when it first surfaced in New York City. The virus reached the United States in one of three ways: in a person infected with West Nile virus, in a mosquito infected with the virus, or in a bird infected with the virus. While no one knows for sure, many experts believe the virus arrived in a migrating bird because bird mortality was especially high that year, implying that birds were sick and dying when they reached New York. When local *Culex* mosquitoes bit the infected birds, they became infected themselves and passed the virus to people and other birds and animals.

Since 1999 the virus has infected at least forty-six thousand people in the United States and killed more than two thousand. It is the most common mosquito-transmitted disease in the nation and has been diagnosed in every state except Alaska and Hawaii. The virus is

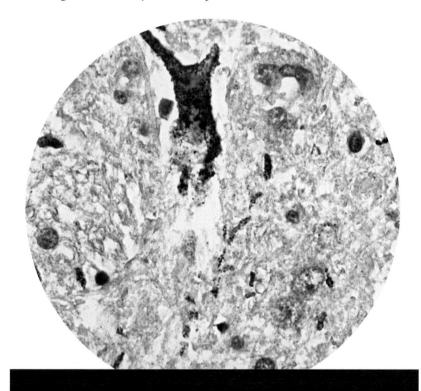

This image of brain tissue from a West Nile encephalitis patient shows infected cells in red. West Nile virus can infect brain cells, damaging these cells and causing encephalitis, coma, and seizures.

common in Africa, Europe, the Middle East, West Asia, and North and South America, making it a near-pandemic disease.

Because 70 to 80 percent of people infected with West Nile virus have no symptoms, it is difficult to know how many people have had it. About one in five people develops fevers, body aches, joint pain, headaches, or rashes. Most people with this symptomatic form recover completely but may experience fatigue and weakness for months.

Less than 1 percent of people infected with the virus develop a serious neurological illness such as meningitis (inflammation of tissues that surround the brain) or encephalitis (inflammation of the brain itself). People with this form may experience severe headaches, high fever, neck stiffness, confusion, coma, seizures, and paralysis. Recovery can take months, and some people never recover fully. Overall, West Nile virus kills about 4 percent of the people it infects in the United States. However, it kills 9 to 10 percent of those who develop meningitis or encephalitis. The virus is also deadly to a wide variety of animals and birds. There is currently no specific treatment for it. Patients receive supportive care such as intravenous fluids and pain medication, if needed.

DENGUE FEVER

Dengue is a reemerging disease in the United States. In the late nineteenth and early twentieth centuries, dengue sickened tens of thousands of people, mostly in southern states such as Texas, Georgia, and South Carolina. Mosquito control programs came into wide use in the 1940s and eradicated dengue-carrying *Aedes* mosquitoes from the United States. Dengue had been absent for nearly seventy-five years. However, *Aedes* mosquitoes were identified in the United States in 2001, probably having reached the country in imported used tires. Dengue has since been diagnosed in Hawaii, Texas, and Florida.

In the twenty-first century, about half the world's population— including many in the United States—is at risk for dengue. As many as four hundred million people develop dengue each year, making it the most common and fastest-spreading mosquito-borne virus in the world. WHO says nearly four billion people in 128 countries are at risk of dengue infection.

Symptoms of dengue include high fever lasting a week, rash, headaches, eye pain, and severe muscle and bone pain. Dengue was once called breakbone fever because of the extreme bone pain. Dengue may progress to dengue hemorrhagic fever (similar to Ebola), with bruising and bleeding. Patients may bleed from the mouth, and blood may appear in the urine and stool. Shock and death can follow. Dengue hemorrhagic fever kills between 10 and 40 percent of those who develop it.

While no specific treatment is available for dengue fever, a new vaccine can help prevent it. The vaccine is for people who are nine to forty-five years old and who live in endemic areas such as Brazil, Indonesia, Vietnam, and Thailand. However, the vaccine reduces dengue cases by only 10 to 30 percent, so doctors have not used it widely. Researchers hope that several other dengue vaccines in development will be more effective.

CHIKUNGUNYA

First identified in Tanzania in 1952, chikungunya has since spread to much of Africa, Southeast Asia, the Caribbean, South and Central America (where nearly seven hundred thousand suspected cases occurred in 2015 alone), and the United States. Between 2006 and 2013, fewer than thirty cases of chikungunya a year were identified in the United States. All were travelers returning from affected areas of Asia and Africa. In 2013 the first local transmission of chikungunya in the Caribbean was identified, meaning that local mosquitoes were spreading the virus to people there. In 2014 US travelers from the Caribbean carried the virus to the United States. Since then local transmission has occurred in Florida, Puerto Rico, and the US Virgin Islands.

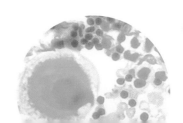

Symptoms of chikungunya are similar to those of dengue fever, so it is difficult to diagnose in regions where both diseases occur. Joint pain may last for months or even years. Serious complications are rare, although chikungunya can lead to death in older patients. No specific treatment is available for chikungunya, nor is a vaccine to prevent it. However, the National Institutes of Health announced in June 2017 that clinical trials to test a chikungunya vaccine for safety would begin later that year.

ZIKA VIRUS

Zika virus hit Rio de Janeiro, Brazil, hard in 2016, infecting more than 26,000 Brazilians between January and June. Hundreds of athletes around the world wondered if it would be safe to attend the Summer Olympic Games there in August. An expert panel for WHO considered whether the Games should be canceled or postponed. However, scientific studies found that the risk of athletes contracting Zika while traveling to Brazil for the Games was low. After the Games, WHO reported that no participating athletes or visitors were known to have the disease.

Zika virus was first identified in the Zika Forest of Uganda in 1947. The virus gradually spread across a narrow band of Africa and Southeast Asia. Fast-forward sixty years to 2007 when Zika hopped across Pacific islands such as Tahiti, Easter Island, and New Caledonia. In 2015 Brazil's first Zika outbreak occurred, and by 2016, Zika had moved into the Caribbean and Florida and Texas.

Former WHO director-general Chan spoke about Zika in 2016 at the 69th World Health Assembly. She said, "The rapidly evolving outbreak of Zika warns us that an old disease that slumbered for 6 decades in Africa and Asia can suddenly wake up on a new continent to cause a global health emergency." She also warned that the world is poorly prepared to cope with emerging and reemerging infectious diseases.

Two types of mosquitoes, *Ae. aegypti* and *Ae. albopictus* (the mosquitoes that reached the United States in the 1960s through used tire imports), carry Zika in the United States. About 60 percent of the American population lives in areas where these mosquitoes thrive. Most mosquitoes must lay their eggs in water. *Ae. aegypti* and *Ae. albopictus* can also lay their eggs on dry surfaces such as the inside of an empty flowerpot, where the eggs remain dormant for up to a year. An infected mother mosquito transmits Zika virus to a few of her eggs. Once hatched, the larvae are already infected with Zika. Scientists know that infected mosquitoes can also pass dengue, West Nile, and yellow fever viruses in their eggs, although it is uncommon.

Infected mosquitoes pass Zika from person to person with their bite. In 2016 researchers also confirmed that the disease can pass from person to person during sexual intercourse. Zika is the only mosquito-borne virus known to be sexually transmitted. Scientists believe this is due to a relatively new mutation in the virus. Zika can also pass through blood transfusions, organ transplants, and from a pregnant woman to her unborn baby.

Eight out of ten people infected with Zika never realize they're sick. Those who develop symptoms typically have fever, rash, joint and muscle pain, pink eye, and headaches. Occasionally, people also develop heart disease or Guillain-Barré syndrome, a disorder of the immune system that weakens and even temporarily paralyzes the limbs. Guillain-Barré is uncommon, but it can occur after other viral diseases, including influenza. However, according to the *New England Journal of Medicine*, Guillain-Barré happens far more often among Zika patients than in people with other viral diseases.

The main fear with Zika is the devastating effect the virus can have on fetuses. Between 10 and 20 percent of babies born to Zika-infected mothers have microcephaly. Babies with this severe birth defect have much smaller than normal brains and heads. Most of these babies never develop normally, and they have a range of serious neurological

Coraliz Dones (*right*) tested positive for Zika when she was seven months pregnant. She sits with other pregnant women at a birth clinic in Carolina, Puerto Rico. In July 2016, the CDC estimated that fifty pregnant women in Puerto Rico became infected with Zika each day.

disabilities. More than four thousand cases of microcephaly occurred in Brazil alone during 2015 and early 2016. Since then cases of both Zika and microcephaly in Brazil and other countries in South and Central America and the Caribbean have dramatically declined. Cases of Zika may be going down because large numbers of people have recovered from it and are now immune to the virus.

While no specific treatment is available for Zika, trials are in progress for several experimental vaccines to prevent it. A study of one of these vaccines showed the vaccine completely protected mice and monkeys against the virus. Human trials began late in 2016. "A safe and effective vaccine to prevent Zika virus infection and the devastating birth defects it causes is a public health imperative," Dr. Anthony S. Fauci, director of the National Institute of Allergies and Infectious Diseases, said. He warns it will be several years before such a vaccine is widely available. Trials are also under way to test a vaccine that targets mosquito saliva. With this new vaccine, the saliva itself—rather than a virus or parasite—will trigger an immune response in the human body to help fight off *any* mosquito-borne disease, including West Nile virus, dengue, chikungunya, Zika, and malaria. Fauci said of this vaccine, "A single vaccine capable of protecting against the scourge of mosquito-borne diseases is a novel concept that, if proven successful, would be a monumental public health advance."

FIGHT THE BITE

Keep mosquitoes away from you! Mosquito bites itch. And mosquitoes that bite you could be carrying one of many transmissible diseases. Fight the bite with a few simple steps:

- Dump out any standing water around your house and yard so mosquitoes don't have a place to lay their eggs. Check outdoor pots, kiddie pools, and anything else that might hold water, especially after it rains. Dump them out too.
- Use window screens, and make sure they don't have holes in them. If your family doesn't have screens, avoid leaving doors or windows open at dusk and dawn when mosquitoes are most active.
- Insect repellents containing the chemical DEET do a good job of keeping mosquitoes off your skin. The US Environmental Protection Agency says DEET is safe for adults and children of all ages. Because the mosquitoes that spread West Nile virus and Zika bite at different times of the day, wear repellent any time you may be around mosquitoes.
- Wear long pants and long-sleeved shirts to keep mosquitoes off your skin. If you live in a warm climate, choose lightweight materials that will also keep you cool.

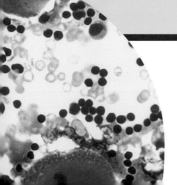

COULD THIS BE THE NEXT PANDEMIC?

Could Zika or one of the other mosquito-borne viruses cause the next pandemic? Probably not. Most mosquito-borne viruses cannot pass directly from person to person. Mosquito-control measures such as cleaning up pools of stagnant water, using mosquito nets, and spraying mosquito breeding grounds with pesticides can greatly slow the transmission of mosquito-borne diseases.

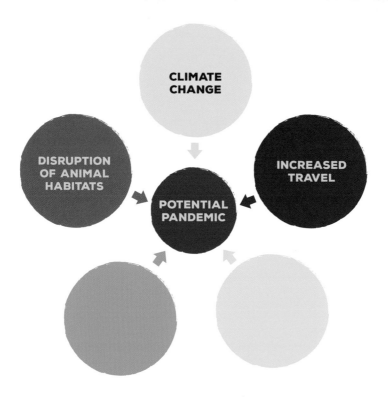

CHAPTER 4

DISRUPTION OF ANIMAL HABITATS

We continue to penetrate the last great forests and other wild
ecosystems of the planet, disrupting the physical structures
and the ecological communities of such places. We cut our way
through the Congo . . . the Amazon . . . Borneo . . . New Guinea and
northeastern Australia. We shake the trees . . . and things fall out.
—David Quammen, science journalist, 2012

Families living in rural, small-town, or remote parts of Liberia
might eat vegetables grown in their own gardens or rice purchased
from a local market. They might hunt in the jungle for meat from
animals such as bats, rats, and chimpanzees. In the United States,

More than 180 species of fruit bats live around the world. These bats are also known as flying foxes. Fruit bats can carry Ebola, Nipah, and other related diseases.

many families build summer cabins deep in the woods. They hire loggers to chop down an acre (0.4 ha) of forest and workers to burn all the vegetation so they can put in a cabin and a lawn.

These Liberian and American families have more in common than you might think. Both live or hunt in areas previously inhabited only by animals and insects. Hunters move deeper into the African jungle, capturing, killing, and eating wild bats and chimpanzees. The diseases those animals carry, such as Ebola, can infect the hunters and, through them, other people. And as builders chop down forests in the United States for new homes and cabins, they and the families who live in the newly opened areas may encounter ticks infected with Lyme disease.

At least 70 percent of new infectious diseases are zoonoses from wild animals. Author David Quammen says, "Mankind's activities are causing the disintegration . . . of natural ecosystems at a cataclysmic rate." These activities include logging, road building, mining, and clearing forests to create cattle pasture, farmland, or new housing. People have destroyed and converted more than half of Earth's natural habitats for human use, according to a 2016 study led by the University of Queensland in Australia. "Almost half of the world's ecoregions now must be classified at very high risk, as 25 times more land has been converted than protected," Dr. James E. M. Watson, one of the study's authors, said. "These highly converted and poorly protected ecoregions occur across all continents, and dominate Europe, south and south-east Asia, western South and North America, western Africa, and Madagascar."

Earth loses about 42 million acres (17 million ha) of natural forests each year. West Africa—where the Ebola epidemic of 2014 began— has suffered extensive deforestation and habitat destruction. Only 20 percent of Guinea's rain forests remain. Liberia has sold logging rights to more than half of its forests. And within the next few years, Sierra Leone will likely have no remaining natural forests. When natural

BAT BASICS

Bats carry many viruses. Yet they are also important creatures in the food chain. For example, insect-eating bats can snap up twelve hundred mosquitoes an hour. They can eat the equivalent of their body weight in insects each night. Bats that eat fruit and nectar help to pollinate flowers, just as bees do. Bats pollinate more than seven hundred different plants, including bananas, avocados, and peaches. Fruit bats are the gardeners of the rain forest, spreading seeds for plants such as figs, palms, and cacao (the source of chocolate) in their feces. People can usually avoid bats by staying out of caves, caverns, and other places where the animals roost. If you do come in contact with a bat, you should never touch it. Do your best to stay away from bats, and they'll do the same for you!

habitats are destroyed and converted to human use, the animals from these habitats come into close contact with people.

BATS HOST VIRULENT VIRUSES

Mosquitoes and ticks aren't the only creatures that carry diseases. Bats are reservoirs (hosts) for more than sixty viruses that can infect people. A reservoir is an animal that carries infectious organisms. The reservoir animal serves as the source of infection for people and other animals. In many cases, bat viruses spill over into human populations when people enter or disrupt bat habitats in some way.

Bats range in size from the flying fox of Australia, which has a 6-foot (1.8 m) wingspan, to the thumbnail-sized bumblebee bat of Thailand. They make up nearly one-quarter of all mammal species. Their great numbers, along with their behavior and mobility, make them the perfect vehicle for spreading viruses. Bats live in densely populated colonies where just a few infected bats can pass a virus to thousands of healthy bats. Their thirty-year life span allows plenty of time for passing viruses to other animals and people. Among the

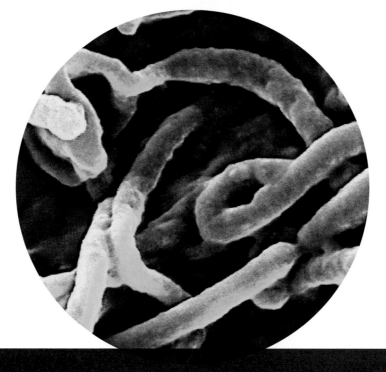

An electron micrograph shows the characteristically hook-shaped Ebola virus on the cells of an African green monkey.

viruses that bats carry are those that cause the following emerging and reemerging diseases that threaten human health:

- **Ebola.** Scientists believe that bats are the natural reservoir for the Ebola virus, which can cause severe hemorrhagic fever with a mortality rate for untreated patients of 80 to 90 percent. West Africa's Ebola epidemic of 2014–2016 likely started when one child in a small village in Guinea handled an infected bat, came down with the disease, and passed it unknowingly to members of his family. Ebola is transmitted through contact with the bodily fluids of an infected person. Bats also carry and transmit Marburg virus, a close relative of Ebola.

- **SARS.** Bats carry the coronavirus that causes SARS. Researchers say that bats passed the SARS virus to animals such as civets by biting them or by contaminating fruit or other food that civets ate. People initially got SARS when they butchered or handled infected civets from Chinese wet markets. Infected people then transmitted SARS to others as they coughed and sneezed. At the time, scientists believed bats could not directly transmit SARS to humans. But a 2013 study found a virus that is closely related to SARS in Chinese horseshoe bats. In the lab, researchers were able to prove that the virus can infect human cells. "This [study] shows that right now in China, there are bats carrying a virus that can directly infect people and cause another SARS pandemic," Peter Daszak, one of the study's authors, said.

- **Nipah virus.** Fruit bats are the reservoir for Nipah. They pass the virus in saliva, urine, and feces. The disease was first identified in Malaysia in 1999 when bats gave the virus to pigs. Humans who worked with infected pigs came down with the virus, and more than one hundred people died. In 2001 people in Bangladesh developed Nipah after drinking wine made from palm tree sap. Fruit bats love this sap and slurp it as it flows into the pots people hang in trees to catch it. Scientists realized that bats were contaminating the sap with Nipah virus. When people drank the contaminated wine, they too became infected. Human-to-human transmission of Nipah was later discovered in several outbreaks in India and Bangladesh. Nipah kills about three-quarters of the people it infects.

CASE STUDY: MIDDLE EAST RESPIRATORY SYNDROME (MERS)

"By all appearances, the camel had a cold," journalist Erika Fry wrote in a 2014 article for *Fortune.com*. "One of nine camels kept in a barn outside Jeddah, Saudi Arabia, the animal was sick and expelling nasal drainage." The camel's owner—a sixty-year-old businessman—did what he could to help. He used his fingers to spread vapor rub inside the camel's nose.

The man soon developed a runny nose and cough. Five days later, he had trouble breathing. His local hospital transferred him to the Dr. Soliman Fakeeh Hospital, a large private medical center in Jeddah. Soon doctors moved him into the hospital's intensive care unit with severe shortness of breath. He developed pneumonia, and his kidneys failed. The man died in June 2012, eleven days after admission to the Jeddah hospital. The camel, however, recovered.

The man was the index patient for MERS. One of his doctors was Ali Mohamed Zaki, a physician who specialized in viruses. As required by law, Zaki sent sputum samples to the Saudi Ministry of Health to check for the dangerous flu known as H1N1. The specimen was negative. After the patient died, Zaki continued to search for the virus's identity. After hitting several dead ends, Zaki discovered the virus was a coronavirus, but it was not SARS. "This was the first evidence that I could be dealing with a novel human coronavirus that had not been described before," Zaki later told a journalist. Zaki sent samples to another lab, which confirmed the new coronavirus. Nearly a year after being identified in 2012, the virus had a new name: Middle East respiratory syndrome.

Scientists linked the index patient (and a few more that soon followed) to close contact with camels. Researchers needed to know more. A 2014 study of camel blood from live camels and from stored samples of camel tissues showed that the virus has been around since about 1992. According to a 2015 article in *Virology Journal*, scientists

A veterinarian draws blood from a camel in Yemen as part of an investigation into the first case of MERS identified there, in 2014. The CDC's Field Epidemiology Training Program, which provides training to help countries locally detect and respond to health threats, led the study.

believe that MERS spilled over from bats to camels about twenty years ago somewhere in East Africa. The article said, "With human activity increasingly overlapping the habitats of bats, disease outbreaks resulting from the spillover of bat coronaviruses will continue to occur." Camels are common in many Middle Eastern and African countries and are used for transportation and for meat and milk. Camels may have gotten MERS from bat droppings or by eating figs and other fruit that infected bats fed on when camels were near them.

Although MERS is not as contagious as SARS, it kills between 30 and 40 percent of the people it infects, compared to SARS's fatality rate of 14 to 15 percent. MERS has reached twenty-seven countries, although most of the cases occur in Saudi Arabia. Most people with MERS have symptoms such as fever, cough, and shortness of breath. In many cases, pneumonia and kidney failure occur. However, some people have no symptoms or only mild coldlike symptoms.

Patients with other medical conditions such as diabetes or heart disease are more likely to die from MERS than are younger, healthier people. According to WHO, as of November 2017, 2,103 laboratory-confirmed cases of MERS have occurred, with at least 733 deaths since the disease was first identified. Person-to-person transmission of MERS is on the rise. This trend worries experts because if person-to-person transmission continues to increase, more people will be at risk of contracting this deadly disease.

EBOLA

A shiny blue thermos arrived at Belgium's Institute of Tropical Medicine in Antwerp in 1976. It could have held enough lemonade for lunch with friends. Or it might have contained coffee for coworkers to share during a break. Instead, it held one of the most dangerous viruses that science would ever identify, floating in a bloody broth of melted ice and test tubes that had broken in transit from Africa.

The blood was from a Belgian nun who worked at a religious mission in Zaire (modern-day Democratic Republic of the Congo). Nuns and patients were dying at an alarming rate at the mission hospital from an unknown disease. In the Antwerp lab, scientists tested the blood and found a virus they had never seen. Researcher Dr. Peter Piot said, "When we saw these worm-like structures under the electron microscope, we were all breathless."

It was Ebola, a new virus—and another zoonosis that had spilled over from animals to people. In tracing the history of the disease, CDC disease detectives discovered that the mission headmaster had returned from a vacation in the jungle, bringing with him dead

A worker with Doctors Without Borders wears protective clothing at an Ebola clinic in Paynesville, Liberia, in 2014.

monkeys for food. He soon became very ill, and the nuns injected him with malaria medication. But he didn't have malaria. He had Ebola. No one knew it yet, but the man had brought Ebola in from the jungle. He soon died, as did his wife. People who attended his funeral became ill and died too. They likely followed the local custom of touching and kissing the dead, later found to be a common way to transmit the virus. People who took care of the headmaster died, and soon the mission nuns noticed an unusually high number of newborns and pregnant women who died. Because medical supplies were scarce, the nuns had used the same syringe they had used to inject the headmaster to give prenatal vitamin injections to pregnant women.

Between 1976 and 2013, Ebola hopscotched around Africa, causing a series of small outbreaks that sickened nearly 2,350 people and killed up to 90 percent of them. Those numbers paled in comparison to the Ebola epidemic of 2014 in the West African nations of Liberia, Guinea, and Sierra Leone. From late December 2013 through March 2016, nearly 28,650 people contracted Ebola and nearly 11,325 died of the disease, most in 2014.

Researchers traced the source of the virus to a small boy named Emile who lived in the tiny village of Meliandou in Guinea. He was the index patient for the Ebola epidemic. Researchers are nearly certain that Emile played with an Ebola-infected bat that was living in a tree at the edge of the jungle near his home. Emile soon died, followed by his pregnant mother. Then Emile's sister Philomena died, as did his grandmother who had taken care of the sick children.

Ebola quickly spread from Guinea into neighboring Sierra Leone and Liberia. The international medical relief organization Doctors Without Borders recognized the threat in April 2014 and tried to warn the world about an imminent epidemic. But it wasn't until August 2014 that Chan, then director-general of WHO, said, "I am declaring the current outbreak of the Ebola a public health emergency of international concern. This is the largest, most severe, most complex outbreak in the nearly four decades history of this disease."

DISEASE PROGRESSION AND TREATMENT

The incubation period of Ebola is two to twenty-one days. Patients are not infectious until they show symptoms. Ebola typically progresses over the course of about two weeks in this way:

- For the first two days after infection, patients experience high fever, body aches, and fatigue.
- Between the third and tenth day, patients have stomach pain, nausea, and vomiting. They may lose large amounts of fluid in watery diarrhea. They can have pain in the bones, chest, and abdomen.

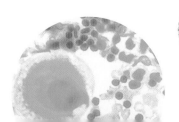

- Most people who die of Ebola do so between the seventh and twelfth day when they go into shock. Fluid leaks from blood vessels into the body, and the kidneys and liver may stop working. Ebola is a hemorrhagic disease, and patients can lose a great deal of blood through vomit and diarrhea and through bleeding into internal organs.
- Most patients who make it through the thirteenth day survive, as their immune system recovers enough to fight the infection.

All bodily fluids from Ebola patients are highly contagious while the patient is ill and after death. In fact, many people caught Ebola while preparing bodies for funerals. Friends and family might kiss or stroke the deceased person, which put them at extremely high risk of developing the disease.

In response to the worsening Ebola epidemic, thousands of health-care workers from around the world poured into West Africa, building hospitals and clinics to care for the critically ill Ebola patients. With no specific treatment for Ebola infection, doctors kept patients hydrated with intravenous fluids. They used medications to control fever and to support the heart and lungs. Most of all, doctors quarantined patients and taught health-care workers and communities to protect themselves with gloves, masks, gowns, and handwashing with a mixture of bleach and water.

When the disease entered the United States, American hospitals treated ten people with Ebola. Most were medical personnel who had cared for Ebola patients. A Liberian man visited family in Dallas, Texas, bringing Ebola with him. Two nurses who took care of him in the hospital got the disease. US health-care workers and hospitals quickly received training and developed protocol for treating Ebola patients.

THE MALARIA MINES OF VENEZUELA

In 2015 twenty-year-old Josué Guevara left college to work in once-abandoned gold mines in Venezuela's remote jungles. The mines pockmarked the jungle with water-filled craters, laced not only with gold but with toxic mercury and malaria-carrying mosquitoes. Venezuela was in a severe economic crisis with plummeting prices for oil, the nation's main export. Like many families there, Guevara and his family desperately needed money. The work in the nation's jungle mines is dangerous and illegal. But in one week, a miner can earn what an average worker in Caracas (the largest city in Venezuela) earns in one month. And sure enough, Guevara uncovered $500 worth of gold in two weeks. During that time, Guevara—like many other miners—came down with malaria.

When Guevara and other malaria-infected miners returned home, they carried the virus in their blood, turning the city mosquitoes throughout Venezuela into malaria carriers. Malaria is overwhelming the cities of Venezuela. Confirmed cases of malaria in 2016 were about 240,000, a 76 percent increase over the previous year. A BBC journalist wrote, "The boom of these illegal mines means more people eroding the rainforest, cutting trees and creating pools of stagnant water to extract gold." That puts people in contact with the mosquitoes that still carry malaria. Locals say, "The environmental impact of mining has . . . 'made mosquitoes angry.'"

As of fall 2017, the government of Venezuela was nearing total collapse with much of the country living in extreme poverty. With little money for medication, bed nets, or insecticides, the nation—once mostly free of malaria—is again overrun with the disease. WHO estimates global malaria deaths plummeted by 62 percent between 2010 and 2015, but time is running backward in Venezuela.

Eighteen-year-old Ender Moreno has been working in Venezuela's gold mines since he was ten years old. He knows the health risks he faces, but he says he will probably continue the work until he dies. He needs the money to help his extremely poor family.

In May 2017, eight people developed Ebola in the Democratic Republic of the Congo, and four of them died. The country was unprepared, treatment was limited, and a promising new vaccine needed further testing before it could be used. Piot, one of the first scientists to see Ebola, said, "Proper isolation of patients . . . plus contract tracing [identifying those who have come in contact with patients] and quarantine should really bring this [outbreak] under control." In July 2017, WHO declared the end of the outbreak in the Democratic Republic of the Congo.

COULD THIS BE THE NEXT PANDEMIC?

Could MERS cause the next pandemic? Possibly. The Saudi Ministry of Health says, "The current medical consensus confirms that the coronavirus that causes MERS is to be found in animal hosts which are camels and bats." If the MERS virus mutates so that it is more easily transmissible between people, it could spread rapidly and kill far more people than SARS did. As with most viral diseases, there is no specific treatment for MERS. Since 2012 the Sabin Vaccine Institute has been working on a vaccine to prevent coronavirus diseases such as SARS and MERS, but it is likely to be years before it is available for humans.

Could Ebola cause the next pandemic? Probably not. Improved health care and public health measures such as quarantine and contact tracing ended the epidemic. Late in 2016, a vaccine to prevent Ebola proved to be extremely effective in preventing the disease. However, the real test of a vaccine happens when the infectious organism is circulating. Ebola doesn't normally circulate in a population. Instead, it periodically spills over from an animal to people. As of fall 2017, the vaccine was awaiting final approval.

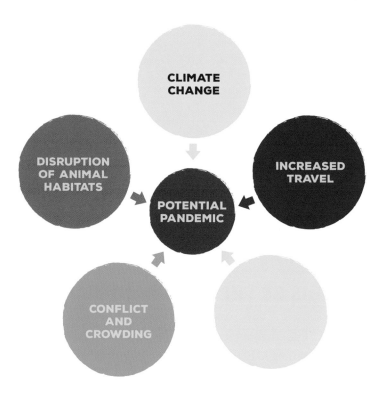

CHAPTER 5

CROWDING IN PEACE AND WAR

*We're more vulnerable [to infectious diseases] because of our
mobility. We're also living more and more in crowded cities. That's
fantastic from the perspective of a virus because in no time it can
infect hundreds of thousands of people.*

—*Dr. Peter Piot, director, London School of Hygiene and Tropical Medicine, 2017*

E very second on Earth, an estimated 4.3 babies are born while
about 1.8 people die, for a net gain of 2.5 more people on our
planet every second of every hour of every day. That means there are
more than 200,000 people added to Earth's population each day.

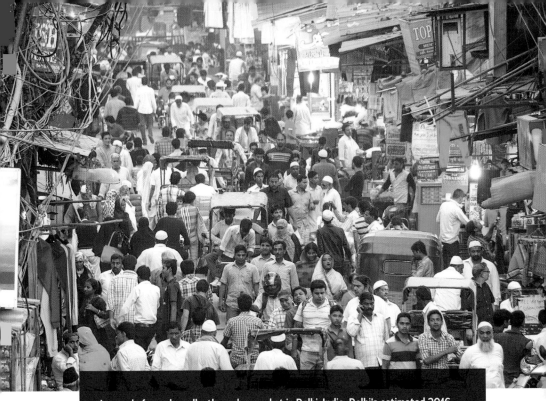

A crowd of people walks through a market in Delhi, India. Delhi's estimated 2016 population was 18.6 million people, and it is expected to grow to 36 million by 2030. An outbreak of dengue in part of Delhi in 2015 sickened more than 15,700 people, overwhelming the city's hospitals.

As of June 2017, the world population is about 7.6 billion people, and the UN expects it to reach 8.6 billion by 2030 and 9.8 billion by 2050. Most of this population growth will occur in Africa and Asia. And with population growth will come an explosion of megacities—cities of ten million or more people. Earth already has twenty-eight megacities, including Tokyo, Japan; Jakarta, Indonesia; Delhi, India; and Seoul, South Korea. The UN predicts the number of megacities will increase to forty-one by 2030.

In Dhaka, Bangladesh, one of the most crowded cities in the world, 114,300 people live in each square mile (2.6 sq. km), compared to 17,000 in San Francisco and 27,000 in New York City. About 1 billion people already live in megacity slums. There, poor housing, insufficient fresh water, and inadequate sanitation put residents at constant risk for illness. The explosive continued growth of the world's population will put even more pressure on food and water supplies and other critical resources—especially health care. Outbreaks of disease may be increasingly difficult to manage.

BUGS IN THE CITY

Crowding contributes to the spread of infectious diseases. Pathogens pass more quickly from person to person than would happen in less crowded environments. In some places, ten people might live in one room, making it easy for one person to infect many others at one time.

In highly populated cities, pathogens are also able to circulate for a much longer time than they do in smaller towns because they have more people to infect. A virus might make nearly everyone in a small town sick in days or weeks before it runs out of people to infect and sputters out. The same virus can circulate for months in a megacity, moving among millions of people, continually finding new victims to infect and possibly mutating into a more dangerous version of the disease during that time. In turn, the millions of infected people infect others, spreading the disease even farther.

Megacities are incubators for disease, exposing a huge number of people in a relatively short time to pathogens. And when the pathogens are new and the population has no immunity, the results can be catastrophic. No More Epidemics said, "A new and highly contagious agent [pathogen] could spread very quickly in packed cities across the globe, killing more than thirty-three million people within two hundred days."

Crowded cities create their own ecosystems. The large numbers of heat-emitting and heat-absorbing factors, such as people and concrete buildings and dark, asphalt pavement, creates warmer temperatures in large cities. In rural areas, with more open space and less heat-absorbing concrete, temperatures are generally cooler. Warming megacities lead to the increased transmission of zoonoses, especially those carried by mosquitoes, which flourish in the warm, densely populated cities.

A 2015 report from the Institute of Medicine said, "The association of dengue [and other viruses] with *Aedes* mosquitoes that live in and around human habitations mean that crowding, poor sanitation, and poverty provide ideal environments for transmission to humans." For example, once the Zika virus reached Brazil in 2015 and established itself in *Aedes* mosquitoes, it spread quickly in the heavily populated slums of Rio de Janeiro. When urban crowding collides with the globe's warming temperatures, the only winners are the pathogens.

DISEASE TRANSMISSION IN WAR TIME

Crowding is a risk factor for disease transmission in peacetime as well as during conflicts. "Wars are among the best incubators of infectious disease," said Dr. Annie Sparrow, a pediatrician and public health expert at the Icahn School of Medicine at Mount Sinai Hospital in New York. Wars destroy communities and their transportation and health-care systems. People flee their homes for safety. Hospitals fall to deadly bombs, and nurses and doctors are killed or flee. "Conflicts in the Middle East and Africa have created the biggest population of refugees and displaced people since World War II [1939–1945]—tens of millions of malnourished people highly vulnerable to new and old pathogens," Sparrow said.

In 2016 the United Nations reported that war and persecution had displaced an astonishing 65.3 million people in 2015 alone, more than half of them children. This number includes refugees (people who leave their homelands to escape war, persecution, or natural disaster) and asylum seekers (people who flee their homelands to escape political persecution for their beliefs and who seek entry into a new, safer country). The number also includes internally displaced people

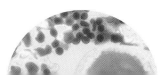

The Dadaab Refugee Complex in Kenya consists of four camps where nearly 245,000 refugees and asylum seekers from East Africa live. In the camp's crowded and underserved conditions, people suffer from lack of clean water, food shortages, and disease from improper hygiene.

(those who flee violence and other conflict but remain within their own countries). Half the displaced people in 2015 were fleeing ongoing conflicts in Syria, Afghanistan, and Somalia. Many of these people end up in massive refugee camps. Uganda, Kenya, South Sudan, and Jordan hold some of the world's largest camps. The camps are very crowded, and often many people share a single tent or living space. Sanitary facilities and medical care may be limited.

In the close quarters of crowded refugee camps, entire populations are exposed to diseases to which they may have no resistance. The European Centre for Disease Prevention and Control found that refugees are especially vulnerable to vaccine-preventable diseases, including measles, chicken pox, polio, diphtheria, meningococcal disease (a dangerous form of bacterial encephalitis and meningitis), tetanus, and influenza. For example, polio and measles have erupted in crowded refugee camps in Syria and Sudan. Conditions in huge camps can also lead to the spread of cholera and tuberculosis, a bacterial lung infection passed from person to person through tiny droplets released by coughing and sneezing.

Refugees are at greater risk for contracting disease because they may have lacked access to routine health care (including vaccinations) for months or years in their own war-ravaged nations. Health-care staff in the camps are often few and underfunded. Supplies such as vaccinations and medications can be difficult to obtain. Vehicles delivering much-needed supplies may not have access to the camps, or the supplies may be destroyed or stolen before reaching their destination.

Disease transmission can also sometimes be a strategy of war. Syria, for example, has been in a brutal civil war since 2011. One organization, Physicians for Human Rights (an organization of scientists and physicians that investigates human rights violations), has documented what it calls the weaponization of disease in Syria. The organization says Syrian government forces are purposefully bombing hospitals and other health-care facilities in areas where people are against the government. The government is also intentionally withholding vaccinations and vital chemicals for water treatment and sanitation. These actions create massive disease outbreaks in the war zones. The people who are able to escape to refugee camps carry those diseases with them and expose others. Syria has not admitted to creating this public health catastrophe.

POLIO, POLITICS, AND WAR

Syria had eradicated polio in 1995. However, after years of conflict in the region, polio reemerged in 2013. The Syrian government said that 99 percent of children had been vaccinated against polio in 2010. In a controversial article published in 2017 in the *Middle East Eye*, a

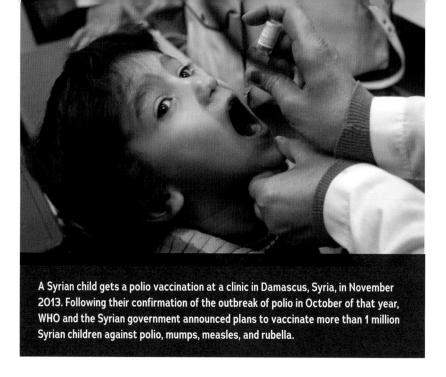

A Syrian child gets a polio vaccination at a clinic in Damascus, Syria, in November 2013. Following their confirmation of the outbreak of polio in October of that year, WHO and the Syrian government announced plans to vaccinate more than 1 million Syrian children against polio, mumps, measles, and rubella.

respected online news service that reports events in the Middle East, Sparrow said the high rate of pre-conflict immunization that Syria claimed was not medically possible.

The spread of polio (and some other diseases) depends on whether herd immunity is present in a population. If 85 percent or more of people are vaccinated against polio, those who do not receive the vaccine are usually protected because others around them can't catch and spread the disease. (Some diseases require higher or lower percentages to protect the population. For example, measles is highly contagious, so 95 percent of the population must be vaccinated to protect those around them.) Sparrow said it takes years for herd immunity to drop and for a disease to begin spreading again. The polio vaccine is believed to provide lifetime immunity from the disease, so if 99 percent of Syrian children had been vaccinated against it in 2010, the disease could not have reemerged in 2013. Sparrow pointed out that new cases of polio occurred almost exclusively in areas that did not support the Syrian government, suggesting that the only children being vaccinated lived in areas supporting the regime.

When polio broke out in July 2013, the Syrian Ministry of Health denied the outbreak for months, saying that WHO's Early Warning Alert and Response System, intended to identify infectious diseases, would have discovered the outbreak if it had occurred. It wasn't until October 2013, after blood samples taken from crippled children were smuggled out of the country and tested elsewhere, that the Syrian government and WHO acknowledged the reappearance of polio in Syria. An international group of health organizations, supported by the Turkish government and the CDC, vaccinated 1.4 million children against polio in those areas of Syria they could reach.

In the *Middle East Eye* article, Sparrow wrote, "It's not just that WHO covers up for the Syrian government's medical misdeeds; it is actively complicit in them." According to Sparrow, those misdeeds include not just the outbreak of polio but also the withholding of supplies and the purposeful bombing of hospitals and clinics.

WHO responded to Sparrow's charges, saying, "Regarding polio, WHO supports the Early Warning Alert and Response System to rapidly detect and respond to disease outbreaks across the country. This is the same system which detected the spread of polio in 2013 and allowed for the swift elimination of the disease."

Sparrow holds WHO partially responsible for polio's return. Elizabeth Hoff is WHO's representative to Syria. Sparrow said, "Hoff's claim that polio was 're-eradicated thanks to concerted efforts by WHO and UNICEF [the United Nations Children's Fund]' is a breathtakingly outrageous attempt to rewrite history and take credit where none is due." Sparrow noted that neither Syria nor WHO's Early Warning Alert and Response System identified the polio cases, and they were not the organizations that vaccinated more than one million children. Rather, independent health organizations in Syria worked with the Turkish government to control the polio outbreak. They had no assistance from WHO or the Syrian government. When it comes to war and politics, only infectious diseases win.

BIOTERRORISM

Bioterrorism is the deliberate release of viruses, bacteria, or other organisms to cause illness or death. People have turned to bioterrorism for thousands of years, mostly to weaken enemies and conquer entire communities. As long ago as 1346, for example, invaders from Mongolia tossed the dead bodies of plague victims into Kaffa (in modern Ukraine) to purposely expose residents to the deadly disease. In 1710 Russians used a similar tactic during a battle with Swedish troops, catapulting the bodies of plague victims at their enemies. During the French and Indian War (1754–1763), British soldiers handed out blankets from smallpox patients to American Indians, hoping to wipe out the Shawnee and Lenape communities. In 1863, during the American Civil War (1861–1865), Confederate (Southern) civilians sold clothing from yellow fever and smallpox victims to Union (Northern) troops. And while no country publicly admits it, several modern nations—including the United States and Russia—developed biological weapons programs during and after World War II.

In the twenty-first century, bioterrorism remains a threat to humanity. The threat is compounded by the possibility that someone could genetically modify an already deadly organism to make it even more lethal. In 1998 Russian scientists reported in a medical journal that they had genetically modified anthrax that may resist current vaccines. The modified anthrax has apparently never been used. The US Army performs its own research on bioterrorism at the Medical Research Institute of Infectious Diseases in Fort Detrick, Maryland. Its work is related only to defensive biomedical research.

The CDC maintains an informational bioterrorism website that describes organisms that could be used in a potential bioterrorism attack and includes information for professionals that discusses how to prepare and plan for bioterrorism emergencies. WHO says the organisms most likely to be used during a bioterrorist attack are anthrax, botulism, plague, and smallpox. Other organisms that could be used for bioterrorism are cholera, Ebola, and several kinds of bacteria that cause food poisoning.

CASE STUDY: CHOLERA

In January 2010, a massive earthquake struck the Caribbean nation of Haiti, one of the poorest nations on Earth. Centered in the country's capital, Port-au-Prince, the powerful earthquake measured a 7.0 magnitude. It killed between 220,000 and 316,000 people, injured 300,000, and displaced 1.5 million. The quake left hundreds of thousands of people living in rubble. Crowding and poor sanitation made a health-care catastrophe almost inevitable.

Aid workers from around the world rushed to Haiti to help. Many were United Nations peacekeepers. UN peacekeepers assist communities during war and natural disaster and help to maintain security and stability. They become involved in politics, train law enforcement officers, and help soldiers, refugees, and other displaced people return to the community. But this time, the UN brought more than workers to Haiti. It also brought cholera.

"I am a young man," Jean-Clair Désir wrote in a letter to the United Nations Security Council in 2015. "In the year 2010, I was a third year student at the University in Agronomy Sciences [in Port-au-Prince, Haiti]. My mother, who meant everything to me, was selling klerin [a beverage made from cane sugar] to pay for my education. [That] year, my mother got cholera on a Tuesday at 11:00 at night. She started vomiting with diarrhea. I made oral rehydration for her, nothing worked. She died at 3:00 in the morning." Désir's mother was one of at least 770,000 Haitians who came down with cholera in 2010 after the massive earthquake.

Four days after his mother's funeral, Désir volunteered at a voting center. He picked up and moved a blue Peacekeeper helmet left in a voting booth, and he said, "Two hours later, I had cholera in the voting center." He recovered from his cholera after receiving intravenous fluids.

The bacteria *Vibrio cholerae* causes cholera. The disease first surfaced two hundred years ago in countries surrounding the Bay

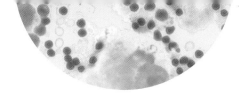

of Bengal, part of the Indian Ocean. Since then cholera has killed millions of people. According to WHO, cholera sickens up to 4 million people in the world each year and kills as many as 143,000. Cholera is most likely to occur when people live in crowded, unsanitary conditions. Without treatment, people may die within hours from severe dehydration resulting from diarrhea. The most common way of getting cholera is through fecal contamination. This occurs by drinking contaminated water or when infected people don't wash their hands properly after using the bathroom.

Haiti had been free of cholera for at least 150 years, so Haitians no longer had natural immunity to the disease. Soon after UN peacekeepers arrived, Haitians began falling ill and dying from cholera. Sewage from a UN camp in Artibonite, about 60 miles (97 km) north of Port-au-Prince, spilled into a river. Within days, hundreds of people downstream developed cholera from the contaminated water. The disease soon spread to the entire country, infecting and killing thousands of Haitians.

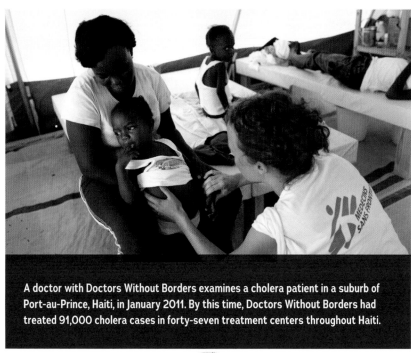

A doctor with Doctors Without Borders examines a cholera patient in a suburb of Port-au-Prince, Haiti, in January 2011. By this time, Doctors Without Borders had treated 91,000 cholera cases in forty-seven treatment centers throughout Haiti.

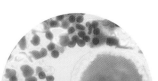

For years the UN denied having any role in or responsibility for the disease outbreak. Yet after an investigation, it became clear that UN peacekeepers were the source. Dr. Daniele Lantagne, a Tufts University environmental engineer, said, "The scientific consensus is that the most likely source was a peacekeeper or peacekeepers." She added that DNA analysis strongly suggests that "this outbreak was probably started by one [individual] or very few infected, asymptomatic individuals—I would guess one."

In 2016, just before he left office as the UN secretary-general, Ban Ki-moon apologized. He said, "On behalf of the United Nations, I want to say very clearly: We apologize to the Haitian people. We simply did not do enough with regard to the cholera outbreak and its spread in Haiti. This has cast a shadow upon the relationship between the United Nations and the people of Haiti."

Since 2010 cholera has sickened at least eight hundred thousand people in Haiti and killed nearly ten thousand. And cholera continues to infect thousands of Haitians each year. In 2013 the first government-led vaccination campaign in Haiti had limited success. However, after Hurricane Matthew in 2016, Haiti launched a massive campaign to vaccinate eight hundred thousand people against cholera after it surged in Matthew's wake. And while the United Nations is trying to raise $400 million from member states to provide assistance for Haitian cholera victims, only a few countries have donated money. According to a 2017 article in *Foreign Policy*, the Trump administration will not approve payment of any money for this purpose.

COULD THIS BE THE NEXT PANDEMIC?

Could cholera cause the next pandemic? Probably not. While large outbreaks such as the one in Haiti may occur in vulnerable nations, improved sanitation in much of the world means fewer people are exposed to the bacteria. Cholera can be prevented with an oral vaccine and can be treated with fluids and antibiotics.

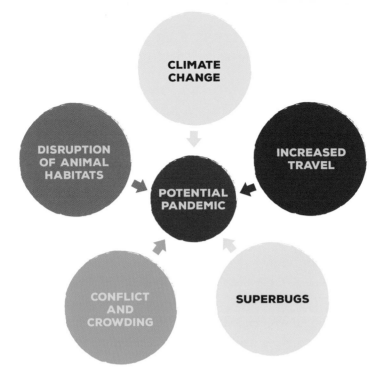

CHAPTER 6

Superbugs on the March

Without urgent action, we are heading for a post-antibiotic era, in which common infections and minor injuries can once again kill.
—*World Health Organization, 2016*

In 1941 fifteen-year-old Arthur Jones huddled in his hospital bed in Oxford, England, shaking with fever. He had developed a life-threatening infection after surgeons had put a steel pin into his femur during an operation. His doctors decided to try an experimental antibiotic called penicillin. The drug was so new that only a few doses existed in the entire world. Scientists at Oxford University were developing the drug, and it took days to make. They had spent seven

Two women work in a lab in Liverpool, England, in 1946. The lab was the largest penicillin factory in the world at the time. In 1940 scientists hired six young English women, later known as Penicillin Girls, to help produce early supplies of penicillin for testing. During World War II, penicillin became widely used to treat soldiers, and many women began working in science and technology to help the war effort.

months building up a supply, and they were now working to test the drug on patients. They worked with doctors at Radcliffe Infirmary to administer the drug.

Forty-three-year-old Albert Alexander was the first patient to receive penicillin for a bacterial infection. He had been working in his rose garden when a thorn scratched his face. The infection spread to his scalp, eyes, and lungs. Pus oozed from his sores. Sulfa drugs, the world's first antibiotics, had failed to help Alexander.

Doctors gave Alexander eight intravenous injections of penicillin on February 12, 1941. His kidneys naturally excreted most of the penicillin in his urine. But the drug was in such short supply that the doctors collected the urine and sent it back to the laboratory. The lab filtered the penicillin from the urine so the doctors could give the drug to Alexander repeatedly. He received the penicillin for five days, and his condition improved greatly.

After Alexander improved, doctors gave all of the remaining doses of penicillin—including the doses taken from Alexander's urine—to Arthur. While Arthur healed, Alexander's condition worsened again. Another round of antibiotics may have saved Alexander, but with no more penicillin available, he died within a few weeks. Arthur, however, survived.

Before antibiotics came into wide use in the mid-1940s, a cut on a finger could lead to a deadly infection. A rusty nail might carry the lethal bacteria that cause tetanus. A person who had surgery might survive the operation but die from a bacterial infection afterward. Bacterial diseases such as diphtheria and scarlet fever often killed children before they were old enough to start school. Others, such as tuberculosis, have killed people for ten thousand years. Pneumonia killed so many elderly people that it was once nicknamed the old man's friend.

The success of antibiotics against disease-causing bacteria is one of modern medicine's greatest triumphs. Penicillin and dozens of other antibiotics have saved millions of lives. By the middle of the twentieth century, antibiotics—along with vaccinations, access to clean drinking water, and improved sanitation—seemed to promise a disease-free life for everyone. Frank Macfarlane Burnet, a virologist and Nobel Prize recipient, said in 1962, "To write about infectious disease is almost to write of something that has passed into history." Burnet spoke too soon.

ANTIBIOTIC RESISTANCE

Disease-causing bacteria have proven more resilient than anyone expected. In fact, infectious diseases have not passed into history. Instead, the bacteria that cause them are becoming increasingly resistant to antibiotics. Known as superbugs, these bacteria are difficult

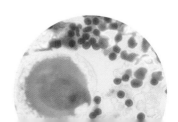

and, in some cases, nearly impossible to conquer. For example, nearly two-thirds of doctors who specialize in infectious diseases have treated patients with infections that did not respond to antibiotics. In 2017 a Nevada woman in her seventies died from an infection resistant to *all* twenty-six antibiotics approved in the United States after returning from a long trip to India, where she had been hospitalized several times and treated for a bone infection in her hip and femur.

WHO says antibiotic resistance is one of the biggest threats to global health. According to the CDC, antibiotic resistance causes more than two million illnesses and twenty-three thousand deaths in the United States each year. Superbugs kill about seven hundred thousand people in the world annually. Experts predict that superbugs may kill ten million people worldwide each year by 2050, far more than die from cancer. Former CDC director Tom Frieden said, "The end of the road isn't very far away for antibiotics . . . we may be in a situation where we have patients in our intensive care units, or patients getting . . . infections for which we do not have antibiotics."

ANTIBIOTICS AT WORK

Most infections pass between people through touch. Bacteria can enter our bodies through cuts in the skin and through mucous membranes in the mouth, eyes, and nose. Bacteria that cause sexually transmitted infections such as gonorrhea enter through the genital area. We drink bacteria in contaminated water and eat them in spoiled food. We also breathe in airborne bacteria, such as the ones that cause tuberculosis.

Once bacteria enter our bodies, they have many ways to make us sick. They multiply quickly and in just hours begin to crowd out and kill host cells. A bacterial cell can become 16 in an hour, more than 250 in two hours, and more than 1 million in five hours. Bacteria kill by stealing nutrients meant for the human body. They release enzymes that break down host cells for food in much the same way our bodies produce enzymes to break down our own food. They also release harmful acids and gases during their normal growth. Some bacteria release dangerous endotoxins into the bloodstream when they die. Endotoxins are extremely dangerous to the human body and can lead to death.

Antibiotics are medications that can cure infections by slowing down the reproduction of bacteria cells or by destroying them altogether. Antibiotics attack bacteria in several ways:

- They can interfere with construction and repair of bacterial cell walls. Without strong cell walls, bacteria burst open and die.
- They can disrupt other cellular processes, such as building proteins, preventing bacteria from multiplying.
- They can prevent bacteria from reproducing by interfering with the creation of DNA or by breaking strands of DNA.
- The drugs can weaken bacteria's ability to take in nutrients and to expel toxins through the cell walls, leading to bacterial death.

THE MECHANICS OF RESISTANCE

Antibiotic resistance can happen quickly. Bacteria may become resistant to new antibiotics within a few months or a couple of years after the medications go into wide use. This is especially true when patients misuse the medications. As a result, patients may experience only a partial cure—or none at all. Bacteria can develop antibiotic-resistant genes in at least four ways:

Random genetic mutation. When bacterial cells divide, they copy their DNA so that each daughter cell has a full set of genetic material, but mutations occur when cells make mistakes. Random mutation can happen as often as once in every ten million bacterial divisions. It may seem as if mutations are rare events, but a single bacterium can produce one billion daughter cells in ten hours. Some mutations keep antibiotics from entering bacterial cells or enable the cells to pump out antibiotics before they can harm the bacteria.

Conjugation. Bacteria can transfer antibiotic-resistant genes to other bacteria of the same or different species during conjugation. During this process, one bacterium's pilus reaches out to another bacterium, creating a pathway between the cells. The plasmid of the first cell moves one strand of its double-stranded DNA into the second cell. Each of the two cells then copies its single strand of DNA so that it has a complete set of genetic material. Very often the DNA carries instructions that make a bacterium resistant to antibiotics. Multiplied by millions of conjugations, resistance can spread widely. Many, but not all, species of bacteria can conjugate.

Transformation. Some bacteria are like microscopic vacuum cleaners, scavenging random bits of DNA left by other species of bacteria or by dead bacteria. If the stray DNA carries antibiotic-resistant genes, the foraging bacterium can become resistant too.

Transduction. Just as viruses can infect people, a group of viruses called bacteriophages (or phages) can attack and infect bacteria. When a phage attacks a bacterium, it adds copies of the bacterium's antibiotic-resistant genes (if present) to its own DNA. Like all viruses, the phage then copies itself many times over, with each daughter virus carrying the antibiotic-resistant genes it originally picked up from the resistant bacterium. As the phages go on to other bacteria, they can transfer the resistant genes to these other bacteria. Transduction creates bacteria with the potential to resist several antibiotics at the same time.

THE MISUSE AND ABUSE OF ANTIBIOTICS

What's happening outside the microscopic world of bacteria that makes antibiotic resistance such a growing danger? The answer is easy: the misuse and abuse of antibiotics. People and animals receive antibiotics

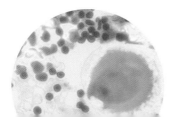

all too frequently. In the United States alone, people and animals consume about 51 tons (46 t) of antibiotics every day. However, the more antibiotics animals and people receive, the more opportunity bacteria have to develop resistance to those drugs.

Of the antibiotics used in the United States, only about 20 percent goes to people. The rest goes to animals. Often those antibiotics are unnecessary or are used incorrectly. For example, antibiotics will not cure infections caused by viruses. Yet people often demand antibiotics for viral diseases such as colds and the flu anyway. Busy doctors may lack the time and energy to educate them about whether antibiotics are appropriate for their condition. A study published by the American Psychological Association in 2017 found that doctors prescribe antibiotics more often to patients who expect to receive them. In fact, five out of six Americans receive a prescription for antibiotics every year, although the CDC estimates that one-third of them are unnecessary.

Even when doctors prescribe antibiotics correctly, patients often don't take them as directed. Some people stop their antibiotics when they start to feel better rather than taking the full course of medication. At this point, only the bacteria susceptible to the antibiotic are dead. Some bacteria remain alive and become resistant to the antibiotic. Finishing the course of medication is meant to kill all of them. If the patient chooses not to take all their doses, the resistant bacteria will continue reproducing and spreading their resistance to succeeding generations. When people take antibiotics only when needed—and take them correctly—they are more likely to work when we really need them.

Animals receive about 80 percent of all antibiotics used in the United States. Certain antibiotics have the effect of promoting growth in animals. Since the 1950s, ranchers and farmers have been giving antibiotics to healthy cows, pigs, turkeys, chickens, and farmed fish to make them grow bigger and faster. Bigger animals mean more meat per animal and therefore bigger profits. Most food animals in

In the United States, food animals such as chickens and cattle often receive antibiotics in their feed or drinking water to promote growth and prevent disease. Many animals are kept on antibiotics for their entire lives. This unnecessary use of antibiotics contributes to the development of antibiotic-resistant bacteria.

the United States receive antibiotics at some point during their lives. Those antibiotics are often the same as or very similar to those given to people. Many are sold without a veterinarian's prescription.

Bacteria inside animals develop resistance to antibiotics in the same way that bacteria inside people do. The antibiotic-resistant bacteria inside animals can reach people in several ways. Farmworkers and other people in regular contact with animals may pick up the antibiotic-resistant bacteria unknowingly while working with infected animals. When they sneeze or cough or touch other people, they pass the bacteria to others. The meat from the infected animals carries the resistant bacteria too. If a family or restaurant worker does not handle and cook raw meat properly and thoroughly, the resistant bacteria can spread to those people during food preparation. (Cooking food thoroughly destroys bacteria.)

Animal feces contain resistant bacteria and can be another source of transmission. Heavy rains can carry waste material into nearby wells and rivers. Farmers may unknowingly use water contaminated with antibiotic-resistant bacteria to irrigate food crops. The resistant bacteria move to people who harvest or eat the raw vegetables or fruit.

TOP FIVE SUPERBUGS

The abuse and misuse of antibiotics is a direct cause of worrisome superbugs. Superbug infection doubles or triples the risk of death. In 2017 WHO published its first-ever list of twelve bacterial pathogens that pose the greatest threat to human health. All are resistant to multiple antibiotics. WHO stresses the urgent need for new antibiotics to battle these superbugs. The top five superbugs are the following:

1. *Acinetobacter baumannii* can cause serious infections in the lungs, blood, brain, and urinary tract. It can also lead to extensive wound infections among soldiers injured by explosives in war zones.
2. *Pseudomonas aeruginosa* can cause serious infections nearly anywhere in the body, including the heart, brain, and lungs. It also causes sepsis, a life-threatening condition in which bacteria enter the bloodstream.
3. *Enterobacteriaceae*, sometimes known as CRE (for carbapenem-resistant *Enterobacteriaceae*), is a large group of bacteria including *E. coli* and *Klebsiella* that cause pneumonia, urinary and gastrointestinal tract infections, and sepsis. Frieden said, "CRE are nightmare bacteria. Our strongest antibiotics don't work and patients are left with potentially untreatable infections."
4. *Enterococcus faecium* is a bacterium that normally lives in the gastrointestinal tract of animals and humans. It causes sepsis,

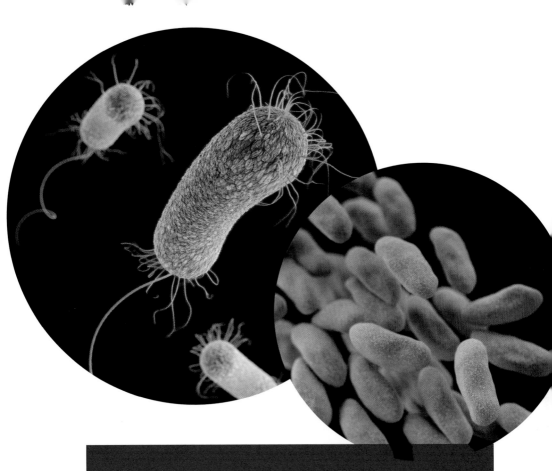

Left: A computer-generated image shows *Pseudomonas aeruginosa* bacteria, which can cause infections in the human bloodstream and urinary tract as well as pneumonia. *Right*: A computer-generated image based on an electron micrograph shows CRE bacteria.

surgical wound infections, and urinary tract infections. It can also infect the heart.

5. *Staphylococcus aureus* bacteria live in the nose and on the skin of 20 to 30 percent of all healthy people. *S. aureus* causes many common skin infections such as boils and blisters, some more serious than others. The most dangerous variety of *S. aureus* is methicillin-resistant *Staph aureus*, or MRSA. *S. aureus* is also resistant to other antibiotics.

CASE STUDY: MRSA

Nine-year-old Brock Wade fell off his scooter at camp and got a bad case of road rash on his leg. A few days later, he was in pediatric intensive care, receiving five different antibiotics for a severe bone infection.

Eleven-year-old Addie Rerecich, who loved to swim and run track, complained of pain in her hip. Doctors sent Addie home from the emergency room even though she had a high fever. Two days later, she entered the hospital and spent five months there, receiving treatment for an infection that had invaded her lungs, muscles, and blood.

Twelve-year-old Carlos Don, who played football and raced motocross, attended a four-day camp. He came home with a high fever. The next day, he was coughing and had problems breathing. Carlos ended up in the hospital, hooked to a breathing machine to help fight the lung damage caused by a body-wide infection. His lungs, heart, and kidneys failed. Carlos did not survive his infection.

These children all suffered from methicillin-resistant *Staphylococcus aureus* (MRSA). Methicillin is the antibiotic that once cured most *S. aureus* infections. However, those bacteria, which can cause serious and even deadly infections in many parts of the body, no longer respond well—if at all—to methicillin and other powerful antibiotics. The United States has one of the world's highest rates of MRSA, with about ninety thousand infections and twenty thousand deaths each year. The United States has a goal of reducing MRSA infections by 50 percent by 2020.

MRSA often begins with a skin sore or boil that becomes swollen, red, and painful. It may grow larger and drain pus. In other cases, as with Addie and Carlos, a break in the skin is not obvious. People can get MRSA from contact with infected wounds or by sharing personal items such as towels or razors that have touched infected skin. The risk for MRSA infection increases when people engage in activities that involve crowding, skin-to-skin contact, and shared equipment.

The National Institute of Allergy and Infectious Disease created this micrograph image, which shows several yellow MRSA bacteria as the blue-colored white blood cell ingests them.

Athletes, students, prison inmates, and military personnel living in barracks are especially susceptible.

What to do? Decrease the risk of MRSA by not sharing personal items, by washing your hands with soap often, and by keeping any skin sores covered with clean, dry bandages. Follow your doctor's advice about how to care properly for any wounds, and always seek medical care for any unexplained fever, muscle or bone pain, or breathing problems.

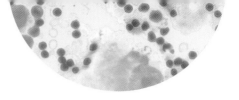

WHAT'S THE PLAN?

Scientists, researchers, and public health leaders are developing plans to help curb the growth of superbugs. For example, an influential report issued by the Review on Antimicrobial Resistance in 2016 calls for a massive public awareness campaign to reduce the global demand for antibiotics for people and animals. The Pew Charitable Trusts Antibiotic Resistance Project and WHO focus on better understanding antibiotic use in humans and animals and on the need to develop new and effective antibiotics. They have come up with several recommendations for use in both humans and animals.

For humans, physicians must be more cautious in their antibiotic-prescribing practices. In 2015 the White House Forum on Antibiotic Stewardship set a goal for 2020 of reducing inappropriate antibiotic prescriptions in doctors' offices by 50 percent and by 20 percent in hospitals. Hospitals, surgery centers, and nursing homes must better control infectious diseases so that people need antibiotics less often.

Some experts are pushing for hospitals to change their policies so that only infectious disease specialists can prescribe antibiotics. Physicians also may use one of the new apps available to help them select the best antibiotic for the patient's condition. The apps offer updated information on antibiotic-resistant bacteria. Dr. Keith Hamilton, director of Antibiotic Stewardship at the Hospital of the University of Pennsylvania, said, "Predicting and understanding the trends and patterns of resistance allows clinicians to choose appropriate medications to treat a patient's infection, and provides the health system real, actionable data to make broad recommendations for use of these life-saving drugs."

Most hospitals have infection control nurses who work with an infection control committee composed of physicians and pharmacists to monitor infections and antibiotic use. When antibiotics are truly called for, doctors, nurses, and pharmacists must be sure to instruct patients about how to use them correctly. Health-care facilities often have nurses who call patients after they leave the hospital to be sure that patients are taking their antibiotics as prescribed.

Scientists are also working to develop better tests to identify pathogens more quickly so that treatment can begin immediately. In 2017 the US government announced ten semifinalists in a multiyear contest to come up with rapid and innovative tests to identify pathogens. The tests specifically combat antibiotic-resistant bacteria.

Experts say antibiotics should be used only to treat sick animals under veterinary supervision and never solely to promote growth. When possible, animals should receive vaccinations against bacterial diseases to reduce the need for antibiotics.

TAKE THEM RIGHT

Never share your antibiotics with another person, and don't stop taking them when you feel better. All medications should be taken exactly as directed by a health-care professional, but it is especially important to do so with antibiotics. In fact, new technology is helping patients to do just that.

The Medisafe Medication Reminder for iOS and Android smartphones is a free app that plays a tune when it's time to take your antibiotic and reminds you when it's time to refill your prescription.

A system called the Tabtime Vibe Vibrating Pill Timer Reminder has compartments for medications and alarms and beeps to let you know when it's time to take your medication.

You can ask for the pharmacy to prepare a pill pack for you that puts medications in their own plastic envelopes in a roll that you unwind each day. You don't have to check the dosage—it has already been figured out for you. You just check the date and time.

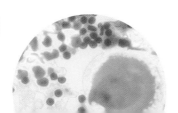

In the past, farmers and ranchers could easily obtain animal antibiotics at feed stores. As of January 2017, the US Food and Drug Administration (FDA, a federal agency that promotes public health by monitoring food and medication safety) mandated that certain antibiotics used by people can no longer be given to healthy animals. A veterinarian's prescription is required to obtain these antibiotics if needed for sick animals. This change does not cover all antibiotics used by farmers and ranchers. But it may help reduce the transfer of antibiotic-resistant bacteria from animals to humans.

Under public pressure, some grocery stores and restaurants are offering food that comes from antibiotic-free animals. For example, in 2016 Consumer Reports, a respected organization that evaluates products and services, gave an A grade to the restaurants Chipotle and Panera Bread for prohibiting antibiotics in all the types of meat they serve. Other fast-food eateries such as McDonalds, Burger King, and KFC are moving toward offering antibiotic-free chicken.

The FDA approved twenty-nine new antibiotics in the 1980s, twenty-three in the 1990s, and only nine in the 2000s. Many of those antibiotics are variations of existing medications. In 2016 Allan Coukell, senior director for health programs at the Pew Charitable Trusts, said, "Drug-resistant bacteria are an ever-increasing threat, but the discovery of new antibiotics has slowed to a crawl. Every antibiotic in use today is based on a discovery made more than 30 years ago."

In September 2017, a major report from WHO about antibiotics said that fifty-one antibiotics were in the clinical pipeline (in some stage of clinical trial), and of those, likely only 14 percent will be finally approved. "Most of the agents in the pipeline are modifications of existing antibiotic classes. They are only short term solutions as they usually cannot overcome multiple existing resistance mechanisms and do not control the growing number of pan-resistant [resistant to all antibiotics] pathogens."

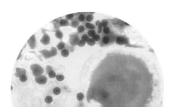

Developing any new drug is extremely expensive and time-consuming, but antibiotics are especially complex. After years of research and tens of millions of dollars, fewer than one out of five antibiotics tested in people is ultimately approved for use. Extensive clinical testing may uncover unacceptable side effects in a promising medication, or the drug may not turn out to be as effective as hoped. Pharmaceutical companies may choose instead to use their financial and human resources to develop new drugs to treat chronic diseases, such as high blood pressure or diabetes. People take medications for

CLINICAL TRIALS

A clinical trial involves research to discover how new medications work in humans. A principal investigator, often a medical doctor or PhD scientist, leads the study. The trials have a research team that includes doctors, nurses, social workers, and other health-care professionals. New prescription medications and vaccines go through clinical trials, the most rigorous type of study, before they are approved for use. A clinical trial has four stages.

In the first stage, the drug is given to a small number of healthy volunteers to determine its safety, dosage, and side effects. In the second stage, the drug is given to a larger group of people with the condition the drug is intended to treat. The research team determines whether the drug is safe and effective to treat the condition. In the third stage, thousands of people take the drug at multiple medical centers. This stage confirms whether the drug is effective, monitors side effects, and compares the drug with other medications that treat the same condition. This stage is randomized and double-blinded—people don't know if they have received a placebo (a pretend medication that will have no effect) or the actual medication. The fourth stage occurs after the FDA has approved the medication. Thousands of people take the drug for years to identify any long-term side effects and to help researchers learn more about how best to use the medication.

KEEPING IT CLEAN

One of the best ways to help prevent infections is by regularly washing your hands with soap and warm water. The humble bar of soap remains one of the greatest weapons in the fight against bacteria. You don't need to use expensive antibacterial soaps advertising that they kill 99.9 percent of germs. In one study, antibacterial soaps actually killed only 46 to 60 percent of bacteria. Not only are the advertising claims false in some instances, but many antibacterial soaps contain an ingredient that may contribute to the development of antibiotic resistance.

Stick to plain soaps, and follow these recommendations:

- Wash your hands before preparing and eating food, and always after going to the bathroom and caring for small children.
- Wash your hands for at least fifteen seconds, time enough to sing the "Happy Birthday" song twice. Scrub your palms, the backs of your hands and wrists, and between your fingers. Remember to wash under your fingernails.
- If you have no running water, alcohol-based hand sanitizers with at least 60 percent alcohol work well.
- Studies have shown that many people don't do a good enough job of washing their hands after visiting public restrooms. To avoid picking up germs those people leave on their hands, always use paper towels to turn off the faucet and to open the bathroom door as you leave.

those disorders for years, unlike antibiotics that are usually taken only for days. While a single dose of an antibiotic may cost far more than a dose of a medication for high blood pressure, the drugs taken for years bring in higher profits to the pharmaceutical companies.

In June 2017, scientists from Rutgers University as well as from Naicons, a biotechnological company, announced a promising new antibiotic found naturally in soil. The experimental antibiotic, known as pseudouridimycin (PUM), killed twenty species of bacteria in lab mice. It is effective against many bacterial infections, some of which are currently resistant to most or all other antibiotics. According to Stefano Donadio, chief executive officer of Naicons, "The discovery also underscores the importance of natural products in providing new antibiotics. Microbes have had billions of years to develop 'chemical weapons' to kill other microbes."

COULD THIS BE THE NEXT PANDEMIC?

Could a bacterial disease resistant to all or most antibiotics cause the next pandemic? Possibly. Bacteria are constantly mutating and becoming resistant to antibiotics. Scientists are constantly discovering new bacterial species. If such bacteria are easily transmitted between people, they could sweep around the globe.

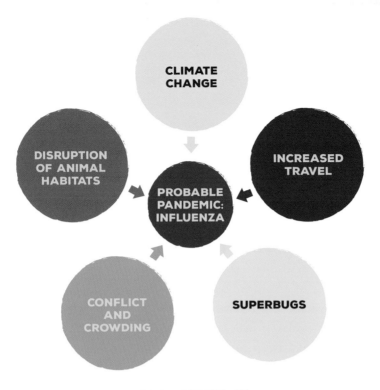

CHAPTER 7

PANDEMIC INFLUENZA

The lead villain in the end-of-the-world pandemic thriller would be everyday influenza, which, with its proven capacity to kill millions, can be spread by a sneeze or a handshake.

—Dr. Ali S. Khan, Department of Epidemiology, University of Nebraska Medical Center, 2016

Chinese government workers donned white coveralls and face masks to prepare for the slaughter. They grabbed chickens, ducks, geese, turkeys, and quail, jammed them into black plastic trash bags, and gassed them with carbon dioxide. When the gas ran out, the workers used knives. It took nearly three days to kill 1.5 million birds.

Workers from the Agriculture and Fisheries department round up chickens at a farm in Hong Kong in 1997. The workers would then kill the chickens using carbon dioxide gas to ensure no chickens infected with H5N1 remained in Hong Kong.

When it was over, Buddhist monks held a seven-day prayer chant for the souls of the dead birds.

The horrific avian massacre was a public health necessity. The new influenza virus, H5N1, had emerged in Hong Kong in 1997. It was so deadly it killed up to 60 percent of the people it infected. The first known case was a three-year-old boy. When he fell ill in May 1997, his doctor told his parents not to worry. But a few days later, the boy went to the hospital with a high fever and pneumonia. He died a week later. Doctors sent blood and tissue samples to the CDC headquarters in Atlanta. Researchers there discovered the boy had died of an avian flu virus that had never been known to infect people.

A teacher at the boy's preschool remembered that the child had played with chicks and ducklings in the school's pet corner. The baby birds died around the same time the boy got sick. Scientists in Hong Kong found that many birds sold in public markets there carried the dangerous virus. The Chinese government then ordered that every bird sold for food in Hong Kong markets be destroyed. World influenza experts believe the mass slaughter may have prevented a pandemic.

Researchers think that H5N1 is one of the deadliest flu viruses yet identified. Two decades later, scattered cases still occur throughout the world, mostly in Asia. Between 2003 and 2016 (the latest year for which there are complete figures), WHO tracked 856 cases in sixteen countries, with 452 deaths. That's not a lot of people, but H5N1's high fatality rate makes it as dangerous as Ebola. "Of all the new pathogens emerging today," science journalist Sonia Shah says, new "influenza viruses like H5N1 are the ones that keep the most virologists up at night."

MEET THE FLU VIRUS

Influenza viruses contain eight strands of RNA held together by a lipid covering. Hundreds of antigens poke out from each virus. The antigens are proteins that stimulate the body's immune system to produce antibodies to ward off infection. When flu viruses with their antigens enter the human body, the body produces antibodies that cause fevers, body aches, and all the other symptoms that go along with flu. Those symptoms are the body's attempt to fight the flu antigens.

Two types of flu antigens allow viruses to enter cells, each with a different job. The first antigen—called hemagglutinin (H)—has spiky points that allow it to latch onto the flu virus's favorite sites, for example cells in the human respiratory tract (the nose, throat, and lungs). Once the virus has successfully docked with a cell in the lungs, more spikes of hemagglutinin grab on to the cell like grappling hooks. Finally, the virus enters the host cell and releases its RNA. As with all

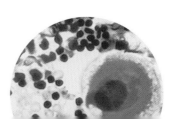

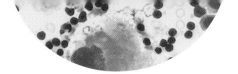

viruses, the genetic material in the RNA hacks the cell's reproductive machinery, forcing it to make millions of daughter viruses.

The second type of antigen, called neuraminidase (N), specializes in helping to spread the infection among cells. Neuraminidase has a boxy head at the end of a stalk that carries enzymes. These enzymes destroy protective chemicals on the host cell's surface. This allows the infected daughter viruses to escape and spread to other cells.

Flu viruses are unstable, and they continually mutate as they pass from person to person. Mutation usually causes only slight changes in a virus, but it happens often enough to allow a virus partially to evade the immune system. The virus is similar to, but not exactly the same, as

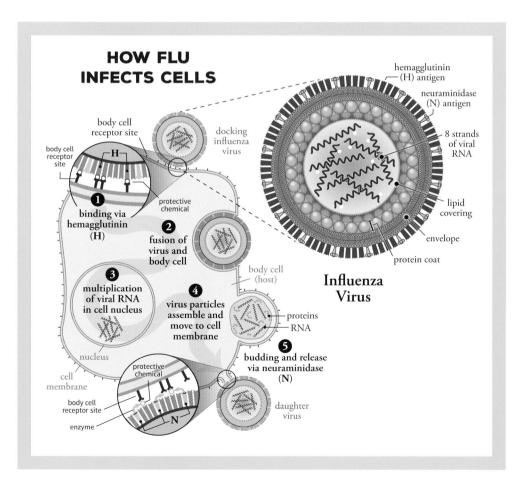

the one from which it mutated. The immune system may not be able to distinguish a virus from its mutation and will therefore not know how to fight the virus.

Scientists call a flu virus's ability to mutate antigen drift. Antigen drift is a relatively minor and gradual change to a virus's genes. The process is slow but continual and is responsible for outbreaks of seasonal flu and smaller epidemics. Antigen drift means that researchers must reformulate the flu vaccine each year to make sure it targets the new flu strains experts expect to occur.

Every few years, major mutations occur. They produce changes in the virus's hemagglutinin, neuraminidase, or both. Called antigen shift, it can occur when two different flu viruses infect a person or a pig at the same time. The viruses reassort—they swap and rearrange their genetic material to create a new hybrid virus. Most people have little or no immune protection when this happens because the immune system does not recognize the new virus and cannot fight it. Existing vaccines are unlikely to be effective.

THE ABCs OF FLU VIRUSES

Scientists have identified three types of flu that infect humans: A, B, and C. Type A is the most common and the most serious. It infects people, birds, and a wide variety of animals, including pigs, cats, horses, and marine mammals. Type B infects only humans and causes milder illness than Type A. Type C infects people and pigs and is very mild. Its symptoms are similar to those of the common cold. Type A flu is divided into subtypes based on the hemagglutinin and neuraminidase antigens in the virus. There are eighteen subtypes of hemagglutinin and eleven subtypes of neuraminidase. The subtypes found in the virus give each flu virus its name. For example, H3N2 was the predominant strain of flu during the 2017–2018 flu season. Types B and C are not subdivided by their antigens.

Each year WHO meets with flu virus researchers to discuss the

A patient receives a flu shot in Los Angeles, California. The flu vaccine causes the body to produce antibodies that will fight infection by the viruses included in the vaccine. About two weeks after receiving the flu vaccine, a person is protected from the viruses targeted by the vaccine.

viruses that are most likely to circulate during the upcoming flu season. WHO then makes recommendations for which viruses to include in the flu vaccine. Each dose of flu vaccine works to prevent two Type A influenza viruses and one or two Type B viruses. The flu vaccination for the 2017–2018 flu season offered protection against H3N2, H1N1, and a B virus. Because Type C is not a threatening form of the flu, a vaccine is not produced for that illness. In the United States, private drug companies make the selected vaccine. The flu vaccine is less effective than many other vaccines, however, because of antigen drift. By the time the vaccine for a particular year becomes available, circulating flu viruses often differ slightly from what WHO and other experts predicted.

Researchers are trying to develop a universal flu vaccine that will work against all strains of flu. Dr. Michael Osterholm, director of the Center for Infectious Disease Research and Policy, said,

"The single most consequential action that we can take to limit, and possibly even prevent, a catastrophic global influenza pandemic is to develop a game-changing influenza vaccine and vaccinate the world's population." He believes this is possible with enough scientific and financial resources.

SKIPPING THE PIG

Like Ebola, Lyme disease, and Zika, influenza is a zoonotic virus. Wild migrating waterfowl, especially ducks and geese, are the source and carriers of flu viruses. In birds the flu virus lives primarily in the intestinal tract, unlike humans and other mammals where it lives in the respiratory tract. Flu viruses don't usually make wild birds sick because they have adapted to the viruses. As the birds fly around the world, their virus-laced droppings fall into ponds, lakes, rivers, and the ocean. Domestic birds such as chickens and ducks pick up the viruses when they drink contaminated water.

Three flu pandemics swept the world in the twentieth century: Spanish flu in 1918 (H1N1), Asian flu (H2N2) in 1957, and Hong Kong flu (H3N2) in 1968. Genetic studies of these viruses suggest that all moved from birds through pigs and then to people. Pigs and people have very similar respiratory tracts. Pigs can contract swine flu, bird flu, and human flu, and viruses from different species can infect a pig at the same time, making pigs a perfect mixing bowl for flu viruses. In a pig's system, bird and pig viruses can swap genes and mutate into new viruses that can infect people. Scientists had no reason to suspect that avian flu viruses could move directly from birds to people, however. This belief changed when H5N1 flu broke out in Hong Kong in 1997. H5N1 skipped pigs entirely, infecting people who had close contact with infected birds.

Another avian flu virus called H7N9 has worried experts since researchers first identified it in China in 2013. As of October 2017, WHO reported that 1,564 people had developed

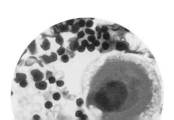

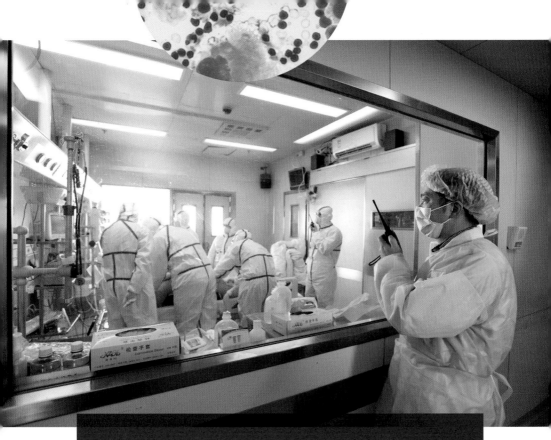

Doctors treat a patient infected with H7N9 in a hospital in China in 2017. During the 2017 outbreak, the Chinese government reported 764 cases of H7N9 with 281 deaths. In fourteen cases, a person passed the disease to at least one other person.

laboratory-confirmed H7N9 and that nearly 40 percent of those patients had died. Actual counts could be higher. Most of the infected people had close contact with infected poultry. H7N9 has moved from person to person in only a few cases.

Dr. Guan Yi, one of the world's leading virologists, has studied H5N1, H1N1, and SARS. Guan, who works in a lab at Hong Kong University, currently focuses on H7N9. He tests chickens from Chinese markets for the virus. Samples of body tissues from both birds and people who died from H7N9 fill his lab. Originally, the virus didn't kill infected chickens, but it mutated and has become deadly to the birds. "Our research shows [H7N9] can kill all the chickens in our lab within 24 hours," Guan said. He fears further mutation of the virus—one that would allow it to easily infect people. "Based on my 20 years of studying H7N9 . . . I'm pessimistic. I think this virus poses the greatest threat to humanity than any other in the past 100 years."

FLU CAN KILL

Think you can't get the flu? Think again. The CDC estimates that twenty-five million Americans caught the flu during the 2015–2016 flu season. Some people who come down with flu say, "It's nothing to worry about. It's just the flu." But more than three hundred thousand Americans were hospitalized because of flu that season, and

COLD OR FLU?

How can you tell if you have a cold or the flu? Here are some common symptoms for each:

Symptoms	Cold	Influenza
Onset of symptoms	Gradual	Sudden
Fever	Rare/mild	Common—can last three to four days
Headache	Rare/mild	Common—may be severe
Body aches	Mild	Common—may be severe
Fatigue, weakness, or both	Mild	Severe—may last for two to three weeks
Cough	Mild/moderate	Common—may be severe
Stuffy nose	Common	Sometimes
Sore throat	Common	Sometimes

about twelve thousand died from flu and flu-related complications such as pneumonia. Flu can kill.

Flu has an incubation period of one to four days before an infected person feels sick. During that time, the person spreads flu viruses as they cough or sneeze. An invisible cloud of flu virus droplets could remain in the air for several hours. People walking through that swarm of airborne viruses can easily catch flu. Meanwhile, flu viruses are busy replicating in the respiratory tract of the infected person. It takes fifty to sixty hours for the viruses to reach critical mass. Then the person realizes they are sick—very sick.

If you catch the flu, you may get a fever of 103° to 104°F (39.4° to 40°C) or more, chills, severe body aches, headaches, sore throat, and extreme fatigue. The body's immune response to flu causes many of the symptoms. For example, fever helps to kill viruses, which are sensitive to increased body temperature, while coughing and sneezing help to expel viruses from the body. Most healthy people recover from flu in ten days or so, although weakness and fatigue can last for two weeks or more. A few people will develop dangerous complications such as pneumonia, meningitis, or Guillain-Barré syndrome.

Antibiotics do not cure flu because it is a virus, and antibiotics only treat bacterial infections. However, doctors can prescribe antiviral medications to decrease the severity of flu symptoms. The FDA has approved three antiviral prescription medications to help treat flu: Tamiflu, Relenza, and Rapivab. The sooner a person starts the medications, the more likely they will work. Antiviral drugs slow down or inhibit viral growth, which can shorten the time a person is sick by one or two days. These drugs also help to prevent serious complications, but they do not cure flu.

The best approach is to prevent flu in the first place. One key step is vaccination. "Even if [the vaccine] is only 30 to 60 percent effective, it sure beats zero protection," Osterholm said. If people do get the flu after being vaccinated, they're not likely to be as sick as

CAN I HELP PREVENT THE FLU?

The CDC recommends some basic precautions to avoid spreading the flu:

- Check with your family doctor about getting your annual flu vaccination. The CDC recommends it for almost everyone over six months of age. The vaccine helps to prevent and to decrease the severity of flu.
- Try to stay away from people who are obviously sick, and stay home if you are sick.
- Cover your cough. Don't cough or sneeze into the air. If you don't have time to find a tissue, cough or sneeze into your bent elbow.
- Wash your hands frequently, especially during flu season.
- Don't share drinks or utensils, especially during flu season.
- Avoid touching your mouth, nose, and eyes. Many cases of flu are passed by touch.
- Eating right and getting enough exercise and sleep can help prevent flu and other illnesses.

someone who is unvaccinated. Vaccination also reduces the risk of being hospitalized for complications of flu such as pneumonia, and when given to pregnant women, protects newborns who cannot be vaccinated.

But not enough Americans get vaccinated. In 2016, for example, only 43 percent of adults and 59 percent of children got vaccinated. Some people don't get vaccinated because they believe—incorrectly—that the vaccine will actually give them flu. "Flu is serious. Flu is unpredictable," former CDC director Frieden said. "Although it is not perfect, the flu vaccine is still our best tool to prevent the flu."

COULD THIS BE THE NEXT PANDEMIC?

Will influenza cause the next pandemic? Many experts believe it will. It's the ideal candidate—an airborne virus easily transmitted from person to person. Could it be a swine flu like H1N1 that surprised the world in 2009? Could it be an avian flu such as H5N1 or H7N9 that mutates to easily infect people? The CDC believes H7N9 has the greatest potential of known flu viruses to cause a pandemic if or when the virus becomes easily transmitted between people through antigen shift. While no one can say for sure when such a pandemic will come, most experts believe it could be soon or as long as a decade or two. In 2017 Osterholm predicted that "a catastrophic influenza pandemic will unfold like a slow-motion tsunami, lasting six to eighteen months."

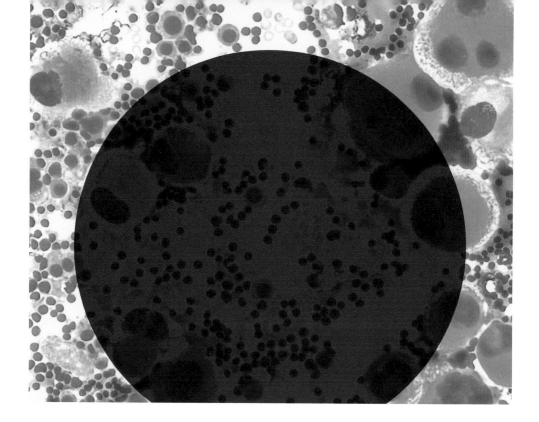

CHAPTER 8

PREVENTING
A PANDEMIC

Outbreaks of infectious diseases are inevitable. Viruses will
continue to jump from animals to humans and spread through the
population. We can, however, prevent outbreaks from turning into
pandemics.

—*Dr. Annie Sparrow, assistant professor of medicine, Icahn School of Medicine at
Mount Sinai, 2016*

The human activities that contribute to the risk of a pandemic
are unlikely to change much in the near future. People will
travel more, not less. Earth will continue warming—at least in the

A CDC worker collects mosquitoes in St. Croix (a district of the US Virgin Islands) to test them for chikungunya. CDC workers have been tracking the spread of chikungunya since 2013, when the first cases of local transmission in the Caribbean region were discovered.

short term. People are likely to continue to clear forests and jungles, disrupting animal habitats and releasing new zoonoses. The human population will keep on growing, causing increased crowding in megacities. Wars will not cease, nor will the need for refugee camps. Superbugs and the diseases they cause are still on the rise, as is the need to develop new drugs and to better monitor and educate people about proper use of antibiotics in people and animals.

WATCH, RESPOND, AND INVEST

In spite of these seemingly overwhelming problems, we have the means to combat and control—to some extent—the risk of a dangerous pandemic. But we need to find the determination and the money to do so. According to Sparrow, the tools to help prevent a pandemic include disease surveillance, rapid response to disease outbreaks, and investment in public health in the most vulnerable parts of the world.

Disease surveillance is the collection and analysis of information that helps to prevent and control infectious disease. For example, the CDC maintains several important surveillance systems that track the health of US citizens:

- Through the CDC's National Vital Statistics System, states collect and share statistics on births, deaths, marriages, and fetal deaths.
- Through laboratory tracking throughout the country, the CDC learns about tuberculosis, HIV/AIDS, influenza, and other illnesses. They also learn about hospital infections such as MRSA and about foodborne and waterborne sicknesses.
- Through the Global Disease Detection program, the CDC helps other countries monitor, detect, report, and respond to health threats around the world.
- States can find data on personal health behaviors through the Behavioral Risk Factor Surveillance System that monitors factors related to preventable illnesses.
- The CDC's National Environmental Public Health Tracking Network monitors trends in health conditions as well as the state of the air, soil, and water to detect threats to health.

Disease surveillance serves as an early warning system to detect potential threats to public health. Yet tracking institutions don't always have enough people or money to do the job. For example, WHO was slow to declare the Ebola epidemic as a Public Health Emergency of International Concern, WHO's status for diseases that require a coordinated international response. In part, the agency did not have enough staff to handle the crisis. A 2015 report in *Newsweek* said,

"Combined with a failure of leadership and accountability at the WHO, the slow response resulted in the 'needless suffering and death' of Ebola patients."

Rapid response requires having medications and vaccines available at clinics and hospitals and pharmacies around the world when they are needed. Teams of epidemiologists, doctors, nurses, medical assistants, laboratory workers, and technology specialists need to be ready to go anywhere in the world on short notice to help people suffering from infectious diseases. For example, Dr. Karlyn Beer is an epidemic intelligence service officer at the CDC. She went to Liberia in September 2014, the month after WHO declared Ebola an epidemic. "I trained health-care workers to safely wear protective suits," she said. "I helped to track and monitor people who were sick or might get sick. I spoke with community and religious leaders about ways they could help their communities to stay healthy." All too often, however, response is

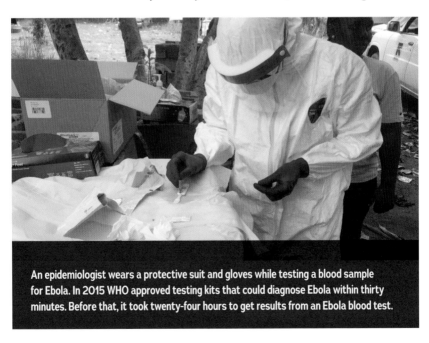

An epidemiologist wears a protective suit and gloves while testing a blood sample for Ebola. In 2015 WHO approved testing kits that could diagnose Ebola within thirty minutes. Before that, it took twenty-four hours to get results from an Ebola blood test.

slow due to factors such as too few human and financial resources, and even geographical challenges such as lack of access to an outbreak due to poor roads or a conflict in the region.

Investment in public health requires having the money to pay for research and medical programs for developing and distributing vaccines, working to reduce infant mortality, and educating people about how to maintain healthy lifestyles. It is much less expensive to prevent disease than it is to care for desperately ill patients who need specialized care.

According to WHO, investing in public health programs saves about four dollars for every one dollar spent on public health. Money from member nations pays for WHO programs, but contributions have not increased for decades. Member nations pay only 25 percent of the cost of running WHO. The remaining 75 percent comes from wealthy individuals, charities, or countries willing to donate more. The Bill and Melinda Gates Foundation, for example, has contributed more for WHO's budget than any organization or government in the world, including the United States.

Scientists are also looking at ways to improve communications among themselves. For example, the International Society for Infectious Diseases publishes a report called *Pro-MED Digest* about infectious diseases in people and animals. This Internet-based reporting system is an informal information-gathering list service that is free and available to anyone who is interested in infectious diseases. Reports are sent out daily to participants around the world, either giving new information about an outbreak or even one case of an infectious disease or asking for more information from other participants. According to the Pro-MED website, "By providing early warning of outbreaks of emerging and reemerging diseases, public health precautions at all levels can be taken in a timely manner to prevent epidemic transmission and to save lives."

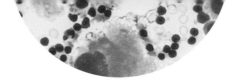

BLUEPRINT FOR ACTION

International organizations large and small are working to help prevent a potential pandemic. For example, a start-up organization called the Coalition for Epidemic Preparedness Innovations (CEPI) focuses on vaccine development. Making new vaccines is extremely time-consuming and expensive, and it is not very profitable for drug companies. The global pharmaceutical market is worth more than $1 trillion. However, the market for vaccines that might prevent a pandemic is only about 3 percent of that total, or $30 billion. That might sound like a lot of money, but to huge companies, it's very little. To make it worthwhile financially, pharmaceutical companies look for partners, incentives, and government support to help pay for developing new vaccines. One such partner is CEPI. It has set a goal of developing vaccines that are safe, effective, affordable, and available at the earliest stage of an outbreak.

"The global response [to an epidemic] often resembles a fire department racing from blaze to blaze," wrote science journalist Donald G. McNeil Jr. "[CEPI] wants something more like a military campaign, with stores of ammunition and different weapons systems [including vaccines] ready to be deployed as soon as a threat emerges."

Early donors to CEPI included the Bill and Melinda Gates Foundation, the governments of Japan and Norway, and Britain's charitable Wellcome Trust. Germany, India, and the European Commission are expected to announce donations too. The United States has not announced plans to contribute. "Ebola and Zika showed that the world is tragically unprepared to detect local outbreaks and respond quickly enough to prevent them from becoming global pandemics," Bill Gates said. "Without investments in research and development, we will remain unequipped when we face the next threat."

CEPI's to-do list targets diseases with the potential to cause large outbreaks. The plan is to have vaccines for each of these priority pathogens before an epidemic strikes:

- Chikungunya
- Coronaviruses (SARS and MERS)
- Filoviruses (the viruses that cause Ebola and Marburg, a disease similar to Ebola)
- Rift Valley Fever (a viral zoonosis that sickens animals and humans, transmitted by contact with the blood and organs of infected animals and by mosquitoes; it can affect the eyes and brain and may cause hemorrhagic fever similar to Ebola)
- West Nile virus

Bringing a new vaccine to market costs as much as $1 billion and can take ten to twenty years. Experimental vaccines for the priority viruses are already in development. After the vaccines are ready, CEPI may also help support research and new vaccines for several other dangerous viruses and for plague, caused by the *Y. pestis* bacteria.

GENETIC SCIENCE AND DISEASE CONTROL

Vaccines are one approach to controlling disease outbreaks. So is genetic modification. For example, researchers are experimenting with ways to kill off malaria parasites in mosquitoes that carry the disease—without killing the mosquitoes themselves. Mosquitoes are an important part of the food chain for other animals, and they are also pollinators, so eradicating mosquitoes is not an option. California scientists have genetically modified mosquitoes that carry malaria so the malaria parasites in their bodies die before the disease passes to people. Dr. Ethan Bier, a biologist involved in the research, said, "If you have a population of 100 million mosquitoes and you released one million of these genetically modified mosquitoes into the same area, the new gene would be spread throughout the entire population in less than a season."

Scientists at a British firm called Oxitec are also working with mosquito genetics. They want to reduce the spread of Zika virus. The scientists modified a mosquito gene so mosquitoes with that gene require the antibiotic tetracycline to survive. The mosquitoes received tetracycline in the lab to keep them alive. When scientists released male mosquitoes with the gene into some areas in Brazil, they mated with wild females and passed the gene to their offspring. These mosquitoes would die before reaching adulthood. This process could cut the wild mosquito population in an area where the genetically modified mosquitoes are released by 90 percent or more, greatly reducing the spread of Zika. As of December 2017, Oxitec scientists were still waiting for approval to release genetically modified mosquitoes in the United States.

A biologist releases genetically modified *Aedes aegypti* mosquitoes in Brazil, hoping to reduce cases of dengue. Scientists hope to see fewer cases of Zika, chikungunya, and yellow fever as they continue releasing and collecting data from genetically modified mosquitoes.

WHAT CAN I DO?

Science writer David Quammen has said, "We should appreciate that these . . . outbreaks of new zoonotic diseases, as well as the recurrence and spread of old ones, are part of a larger pattern, and that humanity is responsible for generating that pattern. We should recognize that they reflect things that we're *doing*, not just things that are *happening* to us." No one person can stop a pandemic, but we can all help in our own way to stop the spread of infectious disease. Here are some ways you can help:

Stay healthy. Every infection that *doesn't* happen is one fewer chance for infections to spread from person to person and from country to country.

Get the proper vaccinations. Vaccines help prevent specific diseases, and they also help limit the spread of antibiotic resistance. For example, people vaccinated against whooping cough are unlikely to get it and are therefore unlikely to need antibiotics to cure it. WHO says that if all children in the world received a vaccine to protect them from becoming infected by one of the bacterial species that cause ear infections, pneumonia, and meningitis, eleven million days of antibiotic use could be prevented each year.

The CDC and the American Academy of Pediatrics recommend that teens get an annual influenza vaccine and two types of vaccine to help prevent meningitis. The meningitis vaccines are required before entering college in some states. Catch-up vaccinations for those not fully immunized as a preteen include the Tdap vaccine to prevent tetanus, diphtheria, and pertussis (whooping cough). They also include vaccines for the sexually transmitted human papillomavirus (HPV) to help prevent genital warts and cancers of the genital tract, throat, and cervix that are caused by HPV.

Reduce your carbon footprint. Just as you leave your footprint when you walk in wet sand at the beach, you leave an invisible carbon footprint with much of what you do. Your carbon footprint represents the total amount of carbon dioxide that your activities produce. Carbon dioxide is the major heat-trapping greenhouse gas responsible for global warming and climate change. Burning fossil fuels such as gasoline and coal to power vehicles, factories, and energy plants is the primary source of carbon dioxide. And the warmer the planet, the more vectors such as mosquitoes and ticks there are to spread disease.

All of us can reduce our carbon footprint. Here are some ideas:

- Walk or take your bike instead of using a car.
- Use mass transit such as buses and trains, or ask friends to carpool.
- Talk to your parents about lowering the heat in your house in the winter. Use fans instead of air-conditioning in the summer. If you do use air-conditioning, raise the thermostat to avoid overcooling. Turn off lights when you leave a room.
- When it's time for a new appliance, urge your parents to buy energy-efficient products.
- Conserve water in the house by using low-flow showerheads and toilets. Don't let faucets run when you aren't using the water. Use drip irrigation in the yard rather than sprinklers. Plant flowers and other plants that don't require a lot of water in the first place.
- Eat locally produced food. About 11 percent of US greenhouse gas emissions come from the transportation of food to market.
- Pack your own lunch and beverages in reusable containers. Eating fast food for lunch is more expensive and less healthy in the long term. Fast food is also heavily packaged with wasteful materials. Putting your coffee in your own colorful thermos is fun and energy efficient.

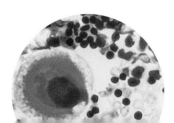

- Reduce, reuse, and recycle. Nearly 30 percent of US greenhouse gas emissions come from manufacturing and transporting consumer goods that we use every day. For example, fossil fuels are used in making plastics of all kinds. Reducing your use of plastics and recycling the plastics you do use is a good way to begin reducing your carbon footprint. So is using less of everything and recycling as much as you can. Work with friends to start a recycling program at your school if you don't already have one. Be creative and see what other ideas you can come up with.

VOLUNTEER FOR HEALTH

You can help prevent mosquito-borne diseases in your own community. Contact your neighborhood association or local parks and recreation board and try starting a program to inspect and clear your neighborhood of standing water where mosquitoes and other insects might breed.

Experts estimate that around the world, one child dies of malaria every two minutes. A ten-dollar bed net can protect a family from mosquitoes that carry malaria. Have a fund-raiser at your school to collect money for Nothing but Nets, an organization that buys and distributes mosquito bed nets to people in countries across sub-Saharan Africa. You could also raise money for the organization by holding a yard sale or a bake sale or collecting and selling recyclables to a recycling center or junkyard. You can arrange a letter-writing or e-mail campaign or an online petition at your school or with your friends to tell your local politicians and other elected officials how you feel about important environmental issues such as climate change.

Teens can volunteer for health-related projects in other countries through church or community groups or organizations such as Projects Abroad. According to the Projects Abroad website, teens

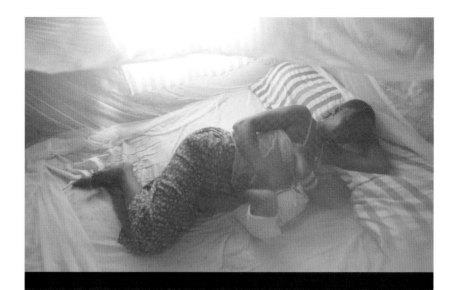

A woman and child sleep under a mosquito net in Sierra Leone. According to Nothing but Nets, 53 percent of the population in sub-Saharan Africa is currently protected by mosquito nets, compared to just 2 percent in 2000. The nets are a simple and affordable way to protect families from malaria and other mosquito-borne diseases.

can learn about medicine and health care in a developing country. They observe local medical staff at work, attend medical workshops about HIV and tropical diseases, and conduct health checkups for children. Teens can also gain practical health-care experience by participating in community outreach programs and running health education campaigns.

Dr. Soka Moses, a young Liberian physician who helped lead his country through the Ebola epidemic, said, "Until the entire world is safe, nowhere is safe." We cannot run away from infectious diseases, and we cannot build a wall high enough to hide from them. But we can all do something. What will you do?

SOURCE NOTES

6 Larry Brilliant, *Unseen Enemy*, first broadcast on CNN, April 7, 2017, 3:40.

22–23 Ali S. Khan, *The Next Pandemic* (New York: PublicAffairs, 2016), 73.

24 Sonia Shah, *Pandemic: Tracking Contagions, from Cholera to Ebola and Beyond* (New York: Sarah Crichton Books, 2016), 51.

26 Mary E. Wilson, "Global Travel and Emerging Infections," a presentation at the Institute of Medicine's workshop, Infectious Disease Movement in a Borderless World, December 16, 2008.

26 Margaret Chan, "World Now at the Start of 2009 Influenza Pandemic," WHO news release, June 11, 2009, http://www.who.int/mediacentre/news /statements/2009/h1n1_pandemic_phase6_20090611/en/.

28 Gro Harlem Brundtland, "World Health Organization Issues Emergency Travel Advisory," WHO news release, March 15, 2003, http://www.who.int /mediacentre/news/releases/2003/pr23/en/.

33 Khan, *The Next Pandemic*, 95.

34 Kim Knowlton, in Molly M. Ginty, "Climate Change Bites," National Resource Defense Council, December 31, 2015, https://www.nrdc.org /stories/climate-change-bites.

35 Gavin Schmidt, in "NASA, NOAA Data Show 2016 Warmest Year on Record Globally," NASA, January 17, 2017, http://climate.nasa.gov/news /2537/nasa-noaa-data-show-2016-warmest-year-on-record-globally/.

36–37 Birgitta Evengard, in Michaeleen Doucleff, "Anthrax Outbreak in Russia Thought to Be the Result of Thawing Permafrost," NPR, August 3, 2016, http://www.npr.org/sections/goatsandsoda/2016/08/03/488400947/anthrax -outbreak-in-russia-thought-to-be-result-of-thawing-permafrost.

38 Alexey Nenyanga, in Tatiana Vasilieva, "If You're Left without Reindeer, There Is Nothing Else," *Greenpeace* (blog), September 16, 2016, http://www .greenpeace.org/international/en/news/Blogs/makingwaves/russia-anthrax -reindeer-indigenous/blog/57511/.

39 Evengard, in Doucleff, "Anthrax Outbreak in Russia."

39 "The Impacts of Climate Change on Human Health in the United States: A Scientific Assessment," US Global Change Research Program, accessed May 1, 2017, 144, https://health2016.globalchange.gov.

40 Ilissa Ocko, "3 Reasons the Zika Outbreak May Be Linked to Climate Change," Environmental Defense Fund, February 16, 2016, https://www.edf .org/blog/2016/02/16/3-reasons-zika-outbreak-may-be-linked-climate-change.

43 "Emerging Viral Diseases: The One Health Connection," Institute of Medicine Forum on Microbial Threats, accessed May 1, 2017, https://www .nap.edu/catalog/18975/emerging-viral-diseases-the-one-health-connection -workshop-summary.

47   Margaret Chan, "Address to the Sixty-Ninth World Health Assembly," May 23, 2016, http://www.who.int/dg/speeches/2016/wha-69/en/.

49   Anthony Fauci, in "NIH Begins Testing Investigational Zika Vaccine in Humans," NIH news release, August 3, 2016, https://www.niaid.nih.gov /news-events/nih-begins-testing-investigational-zika-vaccine-humans.

50   Anthony Fauci, in "Experimental Vaccine Targets Mosquito Saliva," NIH news release, February 21, 2017, https://www.niaid.nih.gov/news-events/nih -begins-study-vaccine-protect-against-mosquito-borne-diseases.

52   David Quammen, *Spillover: Animal Infections and the Next Human Pandemic* (New York: W. W. Norton, 2012), 515–516.

54   Ibid., 40.

54   James Watson, in University of Queensland, "Global Habitat Loss Still Rampant across Much of Earth," *ScienceDaily*, December 7, 2016, https:// www.sciencedaily.com/releases/2016/12/161207092952.htm.

57   Peter Daszak, in Kai Kupferschmidt, "Bats May Be Carrying the Next SARS Pandemic," *Science*, October 30, 2013, http://www.sciencemag.org/news /2013/10/bats-may-be-carrying-next-sars-pandemic.

58   Erika Fry, "CONTAGION—How a Bat Virus Became a Human Killer," *Fortune.com*, August 22, 2014, http://fortune.com/2014/08/22/contagion -how-mers-became-a-human-killer/.

58   Ali Mohamed Zaki, in "The Story of the First MERS Patient," *Nature Middle East: Emerging Science in the Arab World*, June 2, 2014, http://www .natureasia.com/en/nmiddleeast/article/10.1038/nmiddleeast.2014.134.

59   Ben Hu et al, "Bat Origin of Human Coronaviruses," *Virology Journal* 12, no. 221 (2015), https://virologyj.biomedcentral.com/articles/10.1186/s12985-01 5-0422-1.

60   Peter Piot, in "Surviving Ebola," PBS, October 8, 2014, http://video.pbs.org /video/2365340607/.

62   Margaret Chan, "UN Declares Ebola Outbreak Global 'International Public Health Emergency,'" UN News Centre, August 8, 2014, http://www.un.org /apps/news/story.asp?NewsID=48440#.VITWeTHF_To.

64   Daniel Pardo, "The Malaria Mines of Venezuela," BBC, August 24, 2014, http://www.bbc.com/news/health-28689066.

65   Peter Piot, in Jon Cohen, "New Ebola Outbreak Rings Alarm Bells Early," *Science* 356, no. 6340 (May 26, 2017), http://www.sciencemagazinedigital .org/sciencemagazine/26_may_2017?pm=1&fs=1&pg=12#pg12.

65   "Misconceptions about the Coronavirus (MERS-CoV) Debunked," Saudi Arabia Ministry of Health, accessed October 6, 2017, http://www.moh.gov .sa/en/CCC/Misconceptions/Pages/default.aspx.

66   Piot, *Unseen Enemy*, 3:08.

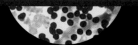

68　"A Call to Action," No More Epidemics, accessed March 5, 2017, 16, http://nomoreepidemics.org/wp-content/uploads/2016/12/A-Call-to-Action.pdf.

69　*Emerging Viral Diseases*, Institute of Medicine Board on Global Health, accessed May 1, 2017, 140, https://www.nap.edu/catalog/18975/emerging-viral-diseases-the-one-health-connection-workshop-summary.

69　Annie Sparrow, "Who Isn't Equipped for a Pandemic or Bioterror Attack? The WHO," *Bulletin of the Atomic Scientists*, June 20, 2016, http://thebulletin.org/who-isnt-equipped-pandemic-or-bioterror-attack-who9555.

69　Ibid.

73　Annie Sparrow, "How a UN Health Agency Became an Apologist for Assad Atrocities," *Middle East Eye*, last modified January 20, 2017, http://www.middleeasteye.net/essays/how-un-humanitarian-agency-becomes-apologist-syrian-government-atrocities-1720133213.

73　MEE staff, "WHO's Response to Dr. Annie Sparrow's Article on Its Work in Syria," *Middle East Eye*, last modified January 20, 2017, http://www.middleeasteye.net/news/whos-detailed-response-dr-annie-sparrows-piece-its-work-syria-1578794339.

73　Sparrow, "UN Health Agency an Apologist."

75　Désir Jean-Claire, letter to the United Nations Security Council, November 30, 2015, http://www.ijdh.org/wp-content/uploads/2015/12/E0061.pdf.

75　Ibid.

77　Daniele Lantagne, in Richard Knox, "Why the UN Is Being Sued over Haiti's Cholera Epidemic," NPR, March 21, 2016, http://www.npr.org/sections/goatsandsoda/2016/03/21/471256913/why-the-u-n-is-being-sued-over-haitis-cholera-epidemic.

77　Ban Ki-moon, in Emanuella Grinberg and Richard Roth, "UN Apologizes for Haiti Cholera Spread in Plan to Eradicate Disease," CNN, last modified December 1, 2016, http://www.cnn.com/2016/12/01/health/haiti-cholera-un-apology/.

78　"Antibiotic Resistance," fact sheet, World Health Organization Media Centre, accessed May 1, 2017, http://www.who.int/mediacentre/factsheets/antibiotic-resistance/en/.

80　Frank Macfarlane Burnet, *Natural History of Infectious Disease* (Cambridge: Cambridge University Press), 1962, 3.

81　Tom Frieden, in Lena H. Sun and Brady Dennis, "The Superbug That Doctors Have Been Dreading Just Reached the US," *Washington Post*, May 27, 2016, https://www.washingtonpost.com/news/to-your-health/wp/2016/05/26/the-superbug-that-doctors-have-been-dreading-just-reached-the-u-s/?utm_term=.588d783d7290.

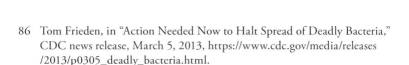

86   Tom Frieden, in "Action Needed Now to Halt Spread of Deadly Bacteria,"
      CDC news release, March 5, 2013, https://www.cdc.gov/media/releases
      /2013/p0305_deadly_bacteria.html.

90   Keith Hamilton, in Katie Wike, "Antibiotic Tracking App, Software
      Being Developed," Health Outcomes, February 20, 2014, https://www
      .healthitoutcomes.com/doc/antibiotic-tracking-app-software-being
      -developed-0001.

92   Allan Coukell, in "Pew Releases Scientific Roadmap to Spur Antibiotic
      Discovery and Innovation," Pew Charitable Trusts news release, May 11,
      2016, http://www.pewtrusts.org/en/about/news-room/press-releases
      /2016/05/11/pew-releases-scientific-roadmap-to-spur-antibiotic-discovery
      -and-innovation.

92   "Antibacterial Agents in Clinical Development," World Health Organization,
      September 2017, http://www.who.int/medicines/areas/rational_use
      /antibacterial_agents_clinical_development/en/.

95   Stefano Donadio, in "New Antibiotic Effective against Drug-Resistant
      Bacteria," *ScienceDaily*, June 15, 2017, https://www.sciencedaily.com/releases
      /2017/06/170615142842.htm.

96   Khan, *The Next Pandemic*, 12.

98   Shah, *Pandemic*, 89–90.

102   Michael T. Osterholm and Mark Olshaker, *Deadliest Enemy: Our War against
      Killer Germs* (New York: Little, Brown, 2017), 301.

104   Guan Yi, in Rob Schmitz, "Why Chinese Scientists Are More Worried Than
      Ever about Bird Flu," NPR, April 11, 2017, http://www.npr.org/sections
      /goatsandsoda/2017/04/11/523271148/why-chinese-scientists-are-more
      -worried-than-ever-about-bird-flu.

105   Osterholm and Olshaker, *Deadliest Enemy*, 91.

106   Tom Frieden, in Rita Rubin, "CDC's Frieden: Flu Vaccine Isn't Perfect, but
      It's the Best Tool We Have to Protect Ourselves," *Forbes*, September 29, 2016,
      https://www.forbes.com/sites/ritarubin/2016/09/29/cdcs-frieden-flu-vaccine
      -isnt-perfect-but-its-the-best-tool-we-have-to-protect-ourselves/#705de587de67.

107   Osterholm and Olshaker, *Deadliest Enemy*, 269.

108   Sparrow, "Who Isn't Equipped?"

111   Conor Gaffey, "Report Slams WHO for Being Too Slow to Respond to
      Ebola," *Newsweek*, November 23, 2015, http://www.newsweek.com/ebola
      -response-who-was-too-slow-report-397384.

111   Karlyn Beer, personal interviews with the author, December 2014.

112   "About ProMED-Mail," International Society for Infectious Diseases,
      accessed October 6, 2017, http://www.isid.org/promedmail/promedmail
      .shtml.

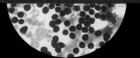

113   Donald G. McNeil Jr., in "Donors and Drug Makers Offer $500 Million to Control Global Epidemics," *New York Times*, January 18, 2017, https://www.nytimes.com/2017/01/18/health/partnership-epidemic-preparedness.html.

113   Bill Gates, in "Global Partnership Launched to Prevent Epidemics with New Vaccines," CEPI news release, January 18, 2017, http://cepi.net/cepi-officially-launched.

114–115   Ethan Bier, in Deborah Netburn, "Scientists Aim to Fight Malaria with Genetically Engineered Mosquitoes," *Los Angeles Times*, November 25, 2015, http://www.latimes.com/science/sciencenow/la-sci-sn-genetically-engineered-mosquitoes-malaria-20151121-story.html.

116   Quammen, *Spillover*, 515.

119   Soka Moses, in *Unseen Enemy*, 1:32:25.

GLOSSARY

antibodies: proteins produced in the body as an immune response to help defend against foreign organisms such as bacteria and viruses

antigen drift: a relatively minor and gradual genetic change to an influenza virus. Antigen drift is responsible for outbreaks of seasonal flu and smaller epidemics, and is the reason why the flu vaccine must be reformulated each year.

antigens: the proteins carried by organisms such as bacteria and viruses that trigger the immune system to send antibodies to destroy them

antigen shift: a sudden radical change to the hemagglutinin and neuraminidase of an influenza virus that produces a new subtype. The immune system cannot recognize the new virus and cannot fight it. Antigen shift is responsible for big epidemics and worldwide pandemics.

bacteria: microscopic single-celled organisms that live nearly everywhere. Some bacteria such as those that cause tetanus, cholera, and Lyme disease are pathogens and can make people sick while other bacteria help produce fermented foods and drinks.

Centers for Disease Control and Prevention (CDC): the US federal agency based in Atlanta, Georgia, charged with protecting Americans from disease, accident, and threats to safety

clinical trials: a series of systematic steps to study how new medications work in humans prior to legal approval of a drug for distribution and sale

coronavirus: a family of viruses that cause SARS, MERS, and some common colds

deoxyribonucleic acid (DNA): the chemical material inside living cells that carries genetic information for most organisms

emerging infectious disease: a disease such as SARS and some strains of flu that are new to people. Other emerging diseases, such as Ebola and Lyme disease, may have occurred for years but went unrecognized or unnamed.

endemic: always present in a region. For example, malaria is endemic in several countries in Africa, including Nigeria, Uganda, and Tanzania.

epidemic: a disease that hits a large number of people in several areas. For example, in 2014 to 2016 scientists classified Ebola as an epidemic because it infected large numbers of people in three countries in West Africa.

hemagglutinin: one of the two types of antigens on a flu virus. Its spiky points allow it to latch onto and enter a cell.

incubation period: the time between exposure to a pathogen such as a flu virus and the appearance of the first symptoms

methicillin-resistant *Staphylococcus aureus* (MRSA): a bacterial infection that could once be easily cured with the antibiotic methicillin, now resistant to methicillin and most other powerful antibiotics

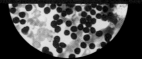

mutation: a random and spontaneous change in an organism's genetic code. Some mutations harm the organism, while others favor it. For example, a mutation may allow a virus that once infected only birds to infect people.

neuraminidase: the second type of antigen on a flu virus. It allows the virus to move between cells, spreading the infection.

outbreak: a disease that strikes a smaller number of people in a limited area, for example, the monkeypox outbreak that appeared in six US states in 2003

pandemic: a disease that infects many people in many parts of the world at the same time. For example, the Spanish flu of 1918–1919 that sickened millions of people around the world was a true pandemic, as is HIV/AIDS.

pathogen: a bacterium, virus, or other microorganism that causes disease

plasmid: a ring of DNA within a bacterial cell that can carry antibiotic-resistant genes from one bacterium to another

reemerging infectious disease: a disease once under control that has become more widespread or resistant to treatment. Examples include cholera and dengue, which are spreading, and malaria and tuberculosis, which are increasingly difficult to treat.

ribonucleic acid (RNA): the chemical material that carries genetic information for certain simple viruses such as Ebola. Bacteria and higher life-forms carry both DNA and RNA. Viruses carry only one or the other. Viruses that carry only RNA are especially vulnerable to mutation.

superbugs: a nickname for bacteria that are increasingly resistant to one or more of the antibiotics that once readily killed them

vaccination: the process of administering a vaccine

vaccine: a chemical substance that stimulates the immune system to produce antibodies against specific organisms, such as the virus that causes influenza or the bacteria that causes tetanus. Doctors typically administer vaccines through injection, although some such as the polio and typhoid vaccines can be given by mouth.

virus: microorganisms smaller than bacteria that cannot grow or reproduce outside of a living cell. Many, but not all, viruses cause diseases in humans and animals.

World Health Organization (WHO): a branch of the United Nations that provides leadership on global health matters and assesses disease trends

zoonosis: an infectious disease such as Ebola, influenza, or Zika that is passed from animals to people

SELECTED BIBLIOGRAPHY

"About Antimicrobial Resistance." Centers for Disease Control and Prevention. Last modified April 6, 2017. https://www.cdc.gov/drugresistance/about.html.

"Antibiotic Resistance." Fact sheet. World Health Organization, October 2016. http://www.who.int/mediacentre/factsheets/antibiotic-resistance/en/.

"Antibiotic Use in Human Health Care." Pew Charitable Trusts, February 2015. http://www.pewtrusts.org/~/media/assets/2015/02/antibioticoveruseinfographic_artfinal_v5.pdf?la=en.

"Avian Influenza H7N9 Virus." World Health Organization. Accessed April 21, 2017. http://www.who.int/influenza/human_animal_interface/influenza_h7n9/en/.

Bichell, Rae Ellen. "Disease Detectives Find a Really Good Reason Not to Drink Date Palm Wine." NPR, March 22, 2016. http://www.npr.org/sections/goatsandsoda/2016/03/22/470803523/disease-detectives-find-a-really-good-reason-not-to-drink-date-palm-wine.

"Chronic Lyme Disease." Lymedisease.org. Accessed April 21, 2017. https://www.lymedisease.org/lyme-basics/lyme-disease/chronic-lyme/.

"Dengue." Centers for Disease Control and Prevention. Last modified January 19, 2016. https://www.cdc.gov/dengue/.

Doucleff, Michaeleen. "Anthrax Outbreak in Russia Thought to Be Result of Thawing Permafrost." NPR, August 3, 2016. http://www.npr.org/sections/goatsandsoda/2016/08/03/488400947/anthrax-outbreak-in-russia-thought-to-be-result-of-thawing-permafrost.

Gillis, Justin. "In Zika Epidemic, a Warning on Climate Change." *New York Times*, February 20, 2016. http://www.nytimes.com/2016/02/21/world/americas/in-zika-epidemic-a-warning-on-climate-change.html?_r=1.

"Highly Pathogenic Asian Avian Influenza A (H5N1) in People." Centers for Disease Control and Prevention. Last modified June 11, 2015. https://www.cdc.gov/flu/avianflu/h5n1-people.htm.

"HIV/AIDS." World Health Organization. Accessed April 21, 2017. http://www.who.int/gho/hiv/en/.

"HIV in the United States: At a Glance." Centers for Disease Control and Prevention. Last modified December 2, 2016. https://www.cdc.gov/hiv/statistics/overview/ataglance.html.

"The Impacts of Climate Change on Human Health in the United States: A Scientific Assessment." US Global Change Research Program, April 2016. https://health2016.globalchange.gov/.

Khan, Ali S. *The Next Pandemic*. New York: PublicAffairs, 2016.

"Lyme Disease Data Tables." Centers for Disease Control and Prevention. Last modified November 21, 2016. https://www.cdc.gov/lyme/stats/tables.html.

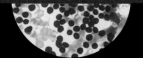

McNeil, Donald G., Jr. "Donors and Drug Makers Offer $500 Million to Control Global Epidemics." *New York Times*, January 18, 2017. https://www.nytimes.com/2017/01/18/health/partnership-epidemic-preparedness.html.

"MERS-CoV Global Summary and Risk Assessment." World Health Organization, December 5, 2016. http://www.who.int/emergencies/mers-cov/mers-summary-2016.pdf?ua=1.

"NASA, NOAA Data Show 2016 Warmest Year on Record Globally." NASA Global Climate Change, January 17, 2017. https://climate.nasa.gov/news/2537/nasa-noaa-data-show-2016-warmest-year-on-record-globally/.

Osterholm, Michael T., and Mark Olshaker. *Deadliest Enemy: Our War against Killer Germs*. New York: Little, Brown, 2017.

"Pew Releases Scientific Roadmap to Spur Antibiotic Discovery and Innovation." Pew Charitable Trusts, May 11, 2016. http://www.pewtrusts.org/en/about/news-room/press-releases/2016/05/11/pew-releases-scientific-roadmap-to-spur-antibiotic-discovery-and-innovation.

Quammen, David. *Spillover: Animal Infections and the Next Human Pandemic*. New York: W. W. Norton, 2012.

Schmitz, Rob. "Why Chinese Scientists Are More Worried Than Ever about Bird Flu." NPR, April 11, 2017. http://www.npr.org/sections/goatsandsoda/2017/04/11/523271148/why-chinese-scientists-are-more-worried-than-ever-about-bird-flu.

Shah, Sonia. *Pandemic: Tracking Contagions, from Cholera to Ebola and Beyond*. New York: Sarah Crichton Books, 2016.

Sifferlin, Alexandra. "The Zika Threat." *Time* 187, no. 18 (2016): 32–41.

Sparrow, Annie. "Who Isn't Equipped for a Pandemic or Bioterror Attack? The WHO." *Bulletin of the Atomic Scientists*, June 20, 2016. http://thebulletin.org/who-isnt-equipped-pandemic-or-bioterror-attack-who9555.

"Surviving Ebola." Transcript of video (not available for streaming) aired on PBS, October 8, 2014. http://www.pbs.org/wgbh/nova/body/surviving-ebola.html.

Tavernise, Sabrina. "No Zika Cases Reported during Rio Olympics, W.H.O. Says." *New York Times*, September 2, 2016. https://www.nytimes.com/2016/09/03/health/zika-rio-olympics.html.

"Tick Removal." Lymedisease.org. Accessed April 21, 2017. https://www.lymedisease.org/lyme-basics/ticks/tick-removal/.

"West Nile Virus." Centers for Disease Control and Prevention. Last modified February 12, 2015. https://www.cdc.gov/westnile/symptoms/index.html.

"WHO Publishes List of Bacteria for Which New Antibiotics Are Urgently Needed." World Health Organization, February 27, 2017. http://www.who.int/mediacentre/news/releases/2017/bacteria-antibiotics-needed/en/.

FURTHER INFORMATION

BOOKS

Barry, John M. *The Great Influenza: The Story of the Deadliest Pandemic in History.* New York: Penguin, 2005. Combining elements of a World War I story and one of the worst pandemics in history, this story of the Spanish flu of 1918–1919 is a fascinating look at the topic.

Fleischman, Paul. *Eyes Wide Open: Going behind the Environmental Headlines.* Somerville, MA: Candlewick, 2014. This book is a wake-up call and action plan to help decode the massive amount of information about the harmful environmental changes under way. Some of these changes are directly related to the increased risk of pandemic.

Goldsmith, Connie. *The Ebola Epidemic: The Fight, the Future.* Minneapolis: Twenty-First Century Books, 2016. Learn where Ebola comes from, how it passes from person to person, and what its symptoms and treatments are. Ebola resulted from human encroachment into animal territories. Can scientists prevent another deadly epidemic in the future?

Gore, Al. *An Inconvenient Truth.* New York: Rodale Books, 2006. The former vice president of the United States and champion for the environment discusses climate change and its consequences for the world in this highly praised book destined to be a classic in the movement to combat global warming.

Haelle, Tara. *Vaccination Investigation: The History and Science of Vaccines.* Minneapolis: Twenty-First Century Books, 2018. Read all about the history of vaccination, the vaccine resistance movement, and the future of vaccine development.

Heos, Bridget. *It's Getting Hot in Here: The Past, Present, and Future of Climate Change.* New York: Houghton Mifflin Harcourt, 2016. Learn the science behind climate change, its history on our planet, and the ways in which humans have contributed to the crisis we face. This book focuses on past human influences, the current state of affairs, and the grim picture for the future.

McNeil, Donald G., Jr. *Zika: The Emerging Epidemic.* New York: W. W. Norton, 2016. *New York Times* science writer McNeil shows us the history of the Zika virus from its first identified origins to its spread in the Americas. Carried by two common mosquitoes, the virus could reach as far north as New England.

Osterholm, Michael T., and Mark Olshaker. *Deadliest Enemy: Our War against Killer Germs.* New York: Little, Brown, 2017. World-famous epidemiologist Osterholm and science writer Olshaker team up to write this fascinating true medical drama about the discovery of known pathogens and the looming threat of a deadly influenza pandemic. Recent outbreaks of Ebola, MERS, and Zika have shown that we are poorly prepared to deal with a pandemic. How can we protect ourselves from dangerous microbes?

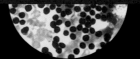

Swanson, Jen. *Geoengineering the Earth's Climate: Resetting the Thermostat.*
Minneapolis: Twenty-First Century Books, 2017. This riveting book looks at climate change and how it affects Earth. This book discusses innovative ways to reverse the trend through different fuels, reforestation, and removal of carbon dioxide from the air.

ORGANIZATIONS AND WEBSITES

Bill and Melinda Gates Foundation
http://www.gatesfoundation.org/
The Gates Foundation has spent billions of dollars improving global health. It focuses on reducing infectious diseases, including malaria, HIV/AIDS, and polio in the poorest parts of the world. The foundation invests heavily in developing new vaccines to prevent infectious disease and new diagnostic testing and drugs to treat them. In some years, the foundation gives more to WHO than any other organization or government.

Centers for Disease Control and Prevention (CDC)
http://www.cdc.org
The CDC's mission is to promote health and quality of life by preventing and controlling disease, injury, and disability. The CDC monitors and investigates health problems around the world and in the United States. Its website offers extensive information about many of the infectious diseases that threaten life and health in the world.

Coalition for Epidemic Preparedness Innovations (CEPI)
http://cepi.net/
CEPI's goal is to work with private, public, and charitable organizations to fund the development of new vaccines. Their challenge is to have vaccines ready before the next outbreak of an emerging or reemerging infectious disease.

Lymedisease.org
https://www.lymedisease.org
This organization works to improve the quality of health care for patients with Lyme and other tick-borne diseases through advocacy, education, physician training, and medical research. Their mission is to prevent Lyme disease, to keep early Lyme disease from becoming chronic, and to obtain access to care for patients with chronic Lyme disease.

Management Sciences for Health
https://www.msh.org/our-work/practice/no-more-epidemics
This organization is an international consortium of governments and agencies with a goal to improve the health of the world's most vulnerable people. A major initiative is No More Epidemics, a five-year global campaign that brings together partners from many fields to work toward better protection from epidemics.

National Aeronautics and Space Administration (NASA)

https://climate.nasa.gov/

NASA and the California Institute of Technology produce and maintain this website, which offers numerous articles, photos, and reports about climate change and how it is affecting the world. The site contains outstanding videos and graphics of an imperiled Earth, a blog, interactive displays, and suggestions for ways to improve the outlook for a healthy planet.

Projects Abroad

https://www.projects-abroad.org/

This organization's mission is to encourage young people to volunteer to work in countries around the world. The site includes extensive information about projects related to health care and medicine in several countries.

World Health Organization (WHO)

http://www.who.int/en/

WHO's goal is to build a better, healthier future for people all over the world. With offices in more than 150 countries, WHO works with governments and other partners to ensure the highest attainable level of health for all people. Its website offers extensive information about many of the infectious diseases that threaten life and health in the world.

World Population Clock

http://www.worldometers.info/world-population/

Based on data updates from the United Nations and US Census Bureau, this informative website counts births and deaths every second in live time. It provides population data by country, density, and religion.

VIDEOS AND AUDIO RECORDINGS

"Genetically Modified Mosquitoes." Howard Hughes Medical Institute video, 8:35, 2016.

http://www.hhmi.org/biointeractive/genetically-modified-mosquitoes

This video talks about Zika and other mosquito-spread viruses in the Americas. One way to genetically modify mosquitoes is to insert a lethality gene that requires the mosquito to receive antibiotic tetracycline to survive. The mosquitoes receive the drug in the lab, but it is not available in the wild. Males are released with the gene, which they pass to wild females, cutting the mosquito population by 95 percent.

"How to Spot Lyme Disease." WebMD News video, 1:01, 2016.

http://www.webmd.com/skin-problems-and-treatments/video/spot-lyme-disease

This short video gives the basics of Lyme disease and the deer ticks that carry it. It shows an excellent example of the bull's-eye rash that 80 percent of people get with a tick bite.

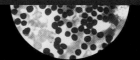

"*Pandemic* Asks: Is a Disease That Will Kill Tens of Millions Coming?" NPR audio
 file, 37:43, 2016.
 http://www.npr.org/programs/fresh-air/2016/02/22/467659069/fresh-air-for
 -february-22-2016
 Fresh Air host Terry Gross interviews Sonia Shah, science writer and author of
 Pandemic: Tracking Contagions, from Cholera to Ebola and Beyond. Shah says that
 90 percent of epidemiologists believe a pandemic that will sicken 1 billion and
 kill up to 165 million is not far off. She links human activities such as human
 encroachment into animal territories and climate change for increasing the risk
 of a pandemic.

"Rise of the Superbugs." YouTube video, 7:23. Posted by It's Okay to Be Smart, April
 15, 2015.
 https://www.youtube.com/watch?v=fyRyZ1zKtyA
 This partially animated film clearly explains what superbugs are, how they
 evolve, and what dangers they pose for our health. Could a simple paper cut be
 deadly in the era of superbugs?

"Think Like a Scientist: Natural Selection in an Outbreak." Vimeo video, 7:30.
 Posted by Day's Edge Productions, 2016.
 https://vimeo.com/188844209
 Narrated by scientists, this film talks about the origin and epidemiology of
 Ebola and how natural selection works in viral mutation during an outbreak.
 It describes how inadequate health-care systems made the situation even worse.
 The film moves from the lab into powerful scenes from the field.

"What If We Killed All the Mosquitoes?" YouTube video, 5:00. Posted by SciShow,
 February 19, 2016.
 https://www.youtube.com/watch?v=e0NT9i4Qnak
 Most mosquito species don't bite humans. Mosquitoes pollinate plants and serve
 as a food source for birds, bats, fish, and other insects. Genetic engineering has
 the potential to eliminate the most harmful of mosquito species—those that
 carry deadly viruses.

"Zika Virus: What We Know (and What We Don't)." YouTube video, 4:22. Posted by
 SciShow, February 5, 2016.
 https://www.youtube.com/watch?v=JUlGN5XJ5dc
 WHO said the Zika virus is spreading explosively across Central and South
 America. Zika has reached the United States as well. When it reached Brazil,
 doctors noticed a huge increase in babies born with microcephaly. Scientists
 worry that the Zika virus may mutate into an even more serious disease.

INDEX

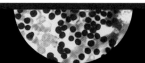

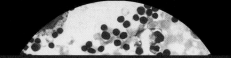

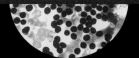

ABOUT THE AUTHOR

Connie Goldsmith has written twenty-two nonfiction books for middle grade and young adult readers and has published more than two hundred magazine articles for adults and children. Her books include *Addiction and Overdose: Confronting an American Crisis; Dogs at War: Military Canine Heroes; Understanding Suicide: A National Epidemic; The Ebola Epidemic: The Fight, The Future* (a Junior Library Guild selection and *Kirkus* starred review); and *Bombs over Bikini* (a Junior Library Guild Selection, a Children's Book Committee at Bank Street College Best Children's Book of the Year, and an SCBWI Crystal Kite winner).

She is an active member of the Society of Children's Book Writers and Illustrators and of the Authors Guild. Goldsmith is a registered nurse with a bachelor of science degree in nursing and a master of public administration degree in health care.

PHOTO ACKNOWLEDGMENTS

The images in this book are used with the permission of: Centers for Disease Control and Prevention Public Health Image Library/James Gathany, p. 7; Centers for Disease Control and Prevention Public Health Image Library/National Institute of Allergy and Infectious Diseases (NIAID), pp. 10, 14, 89; Science Picture Co/Collection Mix: Subjects/Getty Images, p. 11 (black death); Centers for Disease Control and Prevention Public Health Image Library/Jennifer Oosthuizen, p. 11 (enterocolitis); NYPL/Science Source/Getty Images, p. 13; Andrew Burton/ Getty Images News, p. 16; © Laura Westlund/Independent Picture Service, pp. 11(chart), 18, 19, 21, 30, 99; TEH ENG KOON/AFP/Getty Images, p. 25; Centers for Disease Control and Prevention Public Health Image Library, pp. 29, 44, 109; Mike Roemer/Getty Images News, p. 31; Justin Sullivan/Getty Images News, p. 35; Grigorii Pisotsckii/Shutterstock.com, p. 37; Kevin Shields/Alamy Stock Photo, p. 41; Angel Valentin/Getty Images News, p. 49; Wolfgang Kaehler/LightRocket/Getty Images, p. 53; National Institutes of Health/NIAID, p. 56; Centers for Disease Control and Prevention Public Health Image Library/Awadh Mohammed Ba Saleh, Yemen, p. 59; John Moore/Getty Images News, p. 61; JUAN BARRETO/AFP/Getty Images, p. 64; Don Mammoser/Shutterstock.com, p. 67; TONY KARUMBA/AFP/Getty Images, p. 70; LOUAI BESHARA/AFP/Getty Images, p. 72; Jonathan Torgovnik/Getty Images News/Getty Images, p. 76; Daily Herald Archive/SSPL/Getty Images, p. 79; Edwin Remsberg/Photolibrary/ Getty Images, p. 85; Centers for Disease Control and Prevention Public Health Image Library/U.S. Centers for Disease Control and Prevention - Medical Illustrator, p. 87 (both images); LARRY CHAN/AFP/Getty Images, p. 97; Gina Ferazzi/Los Angeles Times/Getty Images, p. 101; STR/ AFP/Getty Images, p. 103; Centers for Disease Control and Prevention Public Health Image Library/John Saindon, p. 111; Victor Moriyama/Getty Images News, p. 115; Ann Johansson/Corbis Historical/Getty Images, p. 119.

Front cover and design elements: David Litman/Shutterstock.com (disease texture); Supphachai Salaeman/Shutterstock.com (map).